The FLAKES *of* WINTER

The FLAKES of WINTER

STAN FISCHLER

Warwick Publishing Inc.
Toronto   Los Angeles

The Flakes of Winter

© 1992 Stan Fischler

Published by the Warwick Publishing Group
Warwick Publishing Inc., 24 Mercer Street, Toronto, Ontario M5V 1H3
Warwick Publishing Inc., 1300 N. Alexandria, Los Angeles, California 90027

Illustrations: George Falkowski
Cover Design: Dave Hader, Studio Conceptions
Text Design: Nick Pitt

ISBN 1 - 895629 - 04 - 7

Distributed in the United States and Canada by:
Firefly Books Ltd.
250 Sparks Avenue
Willowdale, Ontario
M2H 2S4

Printed and bound in Canada

Dedication and Thanks

This book was originally inspired by one person and he deserves full credit. His name is Michael Barnett, a former pro hockey player and now a player's agent of special repute.

Apart from being a great guy, Michael is a terrific idea man. One day in a phone conversation, he regaled me with stories about his favorite hockey cashews. When the laughter simmered down to a roar, Michael opined, "You oughta do a book about funny people in hockey. And I've got just the title for it: the Flakes of Winter."

Egad! Why didn't I think of that? I told Barnett it was a super idea, and he very generously replied, "Well, why don't you go and do it?"

And I did. For that I can thank Jim Williamson of Warwick Publishing who supported me on the project, and editor Nick Pitt who helped see it through.

In addition, I would like to thank the following people for their help in obtaining research and material: Mike Blaze, Joel Bergman, Michael Bourdeau, Roland Burns, Lisa Chenier, Chris Devine, Todd Diamond, Michelle Dye, Sean Farrell, Mark Feinsand, Rita Gelman, Diane Gerace, Robert Gelena, Al Goldfarb, Randy Hu, Jon Jager, Reg Jenkins, Stephan Karasik (my research assistant), Greg Keller, Chris Lemon, Sandra MacPherson, Mary McCarthy, Brian McDonald, Matt Messina (my research editor), Mike Mouat Jr., Alan Rozinsky, Scott Sandell, Eric Servetah, Ashley Scharge, Scott Tracht, Jason Walker, Neil Westcott, and Dave Zafris.

I thank them all.

CONTENTS

INTRODUCTION

The very nature of hockey imbues it with anger.

It has correctly been called a "game of mistakes." These mistakes produce frustration and tension.

Hockey also is a game of physical contact; like involuntarily having a piece of lumber jammed into one's mouth.

That produces anger, a state of mind often associated with the sport.

Then you have referees making calls — good or bad — resulting in still more yelling and screaming.

Get the picture? Hockey can often be an un-humorous bit of business.

And that is why this book has been written.

It is an attempt to convey a single message to the uptight hockey world: *Lighten up!*

With that in mind, I have collected my favorite stories from the past. Some are based on personal experience while often stories come from other sources.

Hockey has always had its share of characters — flakes if you will— and many of these personalities grace the pages of this book.

Despite the tension, hockey is full of laughs and to prove it, a number of ice personalities deliver first-person versions of their favorite rib-tickling incidents and performances.

Hopefully, you'll find it as much fun reading as it was writing about the *Flakes of Winter.*

> Stan Fischler
> New York, New York
> August 1992

Chapter One

OF GOALIES AND RUBBER-ITIS

It has been said, with some justification, that goaltending requires a very special individual; like one who would rather leap out of an airplane as a skydiver than play tennis for an afternoon's enjoyment.

More extreme analysts suggest that anyone who knowingly places his body in front of a piece of vulcanized rubber traveling at speeds in excess of 90 miles per hour simply is nuts. Which leads to the question: do you have to be crazy to be a goaltender?

"I often ask myself that question," says Hall of Famer Chuck ("Bonnie Prince Charlie") Rayner, who tended goal for the New York Rangers in the forties.

In a sense, Rayner answered that question one day when asked what he would do if his son came home and announced that he was going to be a goalie. Rayner replied, "Why, I'd take the big goalie stick out of his hand — and hit him over the head with it!"

More than a few goaltenders have suffered nervous breakdowns or related disorders, often referred to as "rubberitis". Wilf Cude, who played for the Montreal Canadiens during the 1930's, realized that he was suffering from the affliction one afternoon at home when he was having his pre-game steak.

When Cude tried to slice the sirloin he discovered that his wife had under-cooked it to a point where he couldn't cut through it. Furious, Cude picked up the steak and hurled it across the dining room. It slammed into the opposite wall and slowly slipped down to the carpet.

"From the time the steak hit the wall," said Cude, "to the time it finally reached the floor, I realized that I had had enough of goaltending."

Frankie ("Mister Zero") Brimsek knew the feeling. A superb goalie for the Boston Bruins before World War II, Brimsek enlisted with the U.S. Coast Guard and returned to the NHL in 1946. His reflexes dulled, Brimsek never was the same sharp netminder, especially after he was dealt to the inept Chicago Black Hawks in 1949.

One story had it that on the day of a game, Brimsek was walking along a Boston street with a teammate when they approached a corner that had a fire alarm box. In those days each fire stanchion was topped by a red globe which flashed whenever there was an alarm in any part of the city.

As Brimsek and pal reached the corner, "Mister Zero" noticed the flashing red light atop the the fire box. He grabbed his teammate by the arm and shouted "GOAL! GOAL! GOAL! GET ME OUTTA HERE!"

It is a fact of life that the worse a goaltender's defense, the more likely he will be to crack under the strain. Some poor souls, such as the Rangers' Lorne ("Gump") Worsley, resorted to gallows humor to offset the puck stopping pain

After one particularly difficult game during which his defense was especially vulnerable, Worsley was asked by a reporter which NHL team gave him the most trouble. Without hesitation, Gump barked, "the Rangers!"

As if Worsley didn't have enough problems, he was further bothered by one of the most annoying coaches in NHL annals, Phillipe Henri (Phil) Watson, a French-Canadian who suffered a visceral dislike for Gump from the moment they met. Watson thought nothing of needling his netminder and Worsley never hesitated to return the harpoon.

One of the goalie's first ripostes took place after the Rangers had taken a particularly bad beating at Madison Square Garden. With steam coming out his ears, Watson met the media in the press room and suggested that Worsley was drinking too much.

"How can we win," asked Watson, "when our goalie has a beer belly?"

When Watson's put down was rapidly relayed to Worsley, he shot back, "it just goes to show you what a dope we have for a coach. Everyone knows I don't drink beer; just Johnny Walker Red."

The incidents which bedeviled Worsley would have driven anyone to drink. There was for example the 1962 playoff game between the Rangers and the Toronto Maple Leafs. Underdogs in the semi-finals, the Rangers lost the first two games at Toronto but then returned to the friendly confines of Madison Square Garden and stunned the visitors with 5-4 and 4-2 victories. With regained momentum, the Rangers returned to Toronto for the pivotal fifth game of the best of seven series.

The game (played on 5 April 1962 at Maple Leaf Gardens) was a marvelous display of hockey. After three periods of hockey the evenly matched clubs were tied at two. One period of sudden death overtime failed to bring about a decision, which meant another session of pulsating sudden death. It was the Rangers who opened up the attack and seemed on the verge of beating the ancient Johnny Bower in the Toronto goal. But New York fell just short and the Leaf's regrouped, counterattacking shortly after the four minute mark.

Worsley, who had played well throughout the series for New York, was tested on a long shot. He stopped the drive but somehow lost the puck. It feel behind him, directly in front of — but not in — the net. Worsley fell backward, like a man in the act of fainting, and landed with his head on the puck.

Having thwarted the drive, Worsley remained horizontal awaiting the referee's whistle to signal the end of play. One second, two seconds, three seconds passed, and still no whistle. Nevertheless, Worsley was convinced that enough time had elapsed to compel a stoppage of play, so he lifted his head off the rather uncomfortable puck/pillow and prepared to rise for the ensuing face-off.

The face-off never came,

The referee apparently lost track of the puck momentarily and by mistake delayed blowing the whistle. At exactly the moment that Worsley lifted his unprotected head Toronto Center Red Kelly skated across the mouth of the goal, saw the unguarded puck big as life, and quickly pushed it in the net. The red light flashed and the Leafs won 3-2.

Stunned by the setback, the Rangers lost the sixth game of the series, 7-1 and were eliminated from the playoffs.

A Bad Case of Rubber-itis
On March 21, 1991 the Boston Bruins fired 73 shots at Quebec Nordiques goalie Ron Tugnutt. Miraculously the game ended in a 3-3 tie.

The Human Sieve
Perhaps it would be unfair to call Steve Buzinski the worst goalie in NHL history but he didn't get the nickname "Puckgoesinski" for nothing.

The irony of it all is that Buzinski never thought he was all that bad. As a matter of fact, he had a rather lofty impression of himself and was hardly ever daunted by the flashing red light behind him.

It can be said that no goalie ever portrayed the character of the impenetrable ice sphinx better than Steve Buzinski. And nobody ever did it under more difficult circumstances. Buzinski was signed by the New York Rangers shortly after the United States entered World War II. The well of hockey players had nearly run dry. His attitude was unusual to say the least and unrealistic to say the most. But he was a very special character and the Hall of Famers who confronted him found him a great source of amusement.

Unfortunately, Buzinski took himself seriously. For years after he departed the league — almost as quickly as he entered — he steadfastly denied stories told about him. Yet Ranger officials insist they happened, starting just prior to the 1942-43 season.

Lester Patrick, manager of the New York Rangers, sat numb behind his Madison Square Garden desk. It was October 1942, training camp was just a week away and Patrick, for the first time in his lengthy career, did not have a goalkeeper for his club.

Under ordinary circumstances this would have been an incredible state of affairs, but October 1942 was not a normal month. At least not for the National Hockey League.

Canada had been involved in World War II since 1939 and most NHL stars already were in the service. Of all the clubs, the Rangers were the hardest hit. More than half of Patrick's first place 1941-42 club was in military uniform, including goaltender Jim Henry.

Patrick called Frank Boucher, the coach, into his office. "Frankie," he exclaimed, "what are we going to do for a goaltender?"

Boucher was no less puzzled. "The only thing we can do," he replied. "Comb every town in Canada."

The message went out to Ranger scouts across the dominion: "Find a goaltender." Three days later Patrick received a wire from Al Ritchie in Saskatchewan. "HAVE YOUR MAN. WILL REPORT NEXT WEEK. HIS NAME STEVE BUZINSKI."

When the Rangers opened their training camp in Winnipeg, Manitoba the next week, neither Patrick nor Boucher knew very much about Buzinski, the most important man on their team. They had heard he was a grain and cereal expert with the Dominion Experimental Station and a goaltender with an amateur team known as the Swift Current Intermediates.

Buzinski was late arriving at camp. When he finally did make it to the amphitheater the Rangers were already holding a practice skate. "He startled everybody," Boucher recently recalled. "I remember seeing this wee fellow with a black helmet. He was so small all I could see was his head and shoulders over the sideboards. At first I imagined it was the lad who cleaned the ice after a workout. I couldn't help laughing to myself until he climbed the dasher — he only just made it over — and skated to the net. 'Oh, my God,' I said to myself, 'this couldn't be.' But it was. Steve Buzinski had arrived."

He was a little man, thin with extremely bowed legs. He wore a pair of tattered goalie pads that curved around his limbs like cowboy chaps. "When you looked at him," Boucher remembered, "you felt the poor fellow was shot full of holes." But the Rangers were in no position to quibble — there were no challengers. Buzinski was awarded the job by default.

New York opened the season on October 31, at Maple Leaf Gardens in Toronto, and were beaten 7-2. "Steve Buzinski," wrote the Associated Press, "looked flimsy on a couple of goals." Flimsy perhaps, but he did betray an asset, a rare sense of humor.

Midway through the game, Bob Davidson of Toronto fired a shot off Buzinski's forehead during a scramble around the net. The puck inflicted a harmless cut. But as soon as the goalie detected a spot of blood, he swooned to the ice in a dead faint. The Rangers charged at the referee.

"Give Davidson a major penalty for high-sticking," demanded the Rangers' Ott Heller, who was standing over the prostrate Buzinski.

"Take gas," shouted Davidson. "He got hit with the puck!"

"Stick!" wailed Heller.

"Puck!" snapped Davidson.

Suddenly Buzinski opened his eyes, raised his head, and bellowed at the referee: "I got hit with the stick!" And in the same motion, closed his eyes and resumed his reclined position on the ice.

Next stop was Detroit. This time the Rangers lost 12-5.

Carl Liscombe of the Red Wings scored three goals and four assists for a new league record. This feat impressed everyone with the possible exception of Buzinski who marvelled at his own goal-keeping skills. When the Red Wings were leading 7-1, Liscombe fired a shot from center ice. It was considerably wide of the net but Buzinski made a desperate lunge and caught it in the the webbing of his mitt. Then he nonchalantly tossed it into the corner of the rink as teammate Bryan Hextall skated by. "Hex," Buzinski said, with the confidence of a 10-year man, "it's like picking cherries off a tree."

Minutes later, Buzinski gloved another high one. This time a Red Wing skated in front of him, a maneuver which pleased the goaltender no end because it gave him an opportunity to Kibitz with his opponent. Buzinski bobbed and weaved like a welterweight, quipped with the Red Wing and, in the same motion, tossed the puck into the corner — the corner of the net.

Despite the nonsense, Patrick was not about to give up on his rookie, although he had allowed 32 goals in four games. "It isn't fair to pass judgement on Steve after such a short time," Patrick insisted. "Remember, Charlie Gardiner was murdered in his first four games. Then he started to improve and developed into one of the greatest goaltenders in history."

Buzinski was inclined to agree. When a reporter inquired about the difference between big league hockey and the Swift Current Intermediates, Steve was surprised. "No difference at all," he remarked. "Same as back home. Only difference I notice is that the rinks are classier and there are more people than I'm accustomed to see in one game."

But the facts indicated otherwise. On the weekend of November 16, the Rangers were beaten twice by Boston and Buzinski appeared to turn punchy from all the rubber hurled at him.

"Steve showed a new technique," said Dan Daniel in the New York World Telegram. "He adopted the falling system. Persuaded that he who drops over the disk need not have fears of it being elsewhere, Buzinski spent more time on the ice than a mackerel in cold storage."

After the ninth game, the Rangers were in last place and even Patrick was ready to concede that Buzinski was not a major leaguer. Coincidentally, some of the Rangers heard that Jimmy Franks, a goalie of proven ability, was available. They threatened to mutiny unless Patrick replaced Buzinski with Franks. Patrick agreed.

Franks became the Ranger goaltender but Patrick kept Buzinski on the payroll. "He was a refreshing prairie boy," Boucher explained, "always good for laughs. We simply listed him as a member of our public relations department."

The Ultimate Case of Rubber-itis

A number of fans and players have suffered sympathy pangs for the San Jose Sharks goaltending corps. But none can be expected to set a new record for saves in a NHL game.

The ultimate case of "Rubber-Itis" befell a goaltender named Sam Lopresti. On the night of March 4, 1941, Sam Lopresti guarded the Chicago Black Hawk net at Boston Garden and faced an incredible 83 shots on goal! Frank Brimsek, the Boston netminder that night, faced only 18 shots the entire game, while Lopresti met a barrage of 36 pucks in the first period alone, followed by 26 shots in the second and 21 in the third.

More amazing than the amount of shots on goal was the amount Lopresti directed out of danger that night. Only three goals got beyond Lopresti and it wasn't until a late third period score by Bruin Eddie Wiseman that the game was decided. The final score: Boston 3, Chicago 2.

"The Bruins didn't get the winning goal until the end of the game," Lopresti once recalled from his tavern in, Minnesota. "Wiseman got it on a rebound. But we couldn't do anything right from the opening faceoff; just couldn't move the puck out of our zone. They were shooting from every angle and I didn't see half the shots. They were bouncing off my pads, chest protector, my arms, my shoulders. I didn't even know where they were coming from. I lost between eight and 10 pounds that night."

After his second big-league season, the same year Lopresti faced the 83-shot barrage, he joined the United States Navy on the theory that "it was safer to face Nazi U-boats in the North Atlantic than vulcanized rubber in North America."

Pat Quinn's Favorite Goalie Story

Every hockey person I know can come up with a good story that shows you that goaltenders *are* different but I don't know too many who can match the one about Al Smith's instant retirement.

Smitty was a teammate of mine on the Maple Leafs in the late 1960's and also played with Pittsburgh, Detroit and a few other clubs.

He was a good goaltender and like so many of them, he wanted to play as much as possible.

Coaches are funny when it comes to goalies and sometimes they favor one over the other without any real rational basis. And that's where Smitty comes in; he was playing for a coach who wasn't exactly in his corner.

Al hadn't been used very much and with each game he became more frustrated and kept riding the bench.

Finally, there was a game where the club's starting goalie didn't do too well and the coach decided to yank him in favor of Al. The coach turned to him and said, "Okay, Smith, it's your turn to go in."

So Smitty put on his gloves, grabbed his stick and stepped on the ice.

The first thing he did was wave to all the fans; then he skated straight across the ice, but not for the crease as everyone had expected.

Smitty went straight for the players' exit, skated off the ice and headed right for the dressing room.

He took off his equipment and that was it, his farewell.

Everyone in the building kept waiting for him to come back but Smitty never did. That was it; Al Smith was gone!

A Newsman's Analysis of Flakie Goalies

Vancouver Sun columnist Jim Taylor is one of the wittiest and most perceptive hockey journalists on the continent. In an analysis of Canucks goalie Troy Gamble one day during the 1991-92 season, Taylor offered these words about the netminding profession.

"Any discussion of hockey goaltenders must begin with the assumption that they are about three sandwiches shy of a picnic.

"I can prove this.

"From the moment primitive man first lurched erect, he and most who came after him survived on the principle that when something hard and potentially painful comes at you at great velocity, you get the hell out of its path.

"Goalkeepers throw themselves INTO its path. I rest my case!"

The Case of the Missing Mask

The playoff game between the Toronto Maple Leafs and New York Rangers at Madison Square Garden was proceeding normally on April 8, 1971. It was the third period and Toronto nursed a 3-1 lead.

Tempers were becoming frayed and, finally, a melee erupted behind the Toronto net which was guarded by a masked Bernie Parent. As soon as the Leafs' goalie left his crease, Parent's Rangers counterpart, Ed Giacomin, raced from the other end of the rink to even things up.

Eschewing his mask and gloves, Giacomin joined the fray as did Rangers left wing Vic Hadfield who snatched Parent's mask and flipped it into the crowd.

Instead of returning the mask, a Ranger fan who originally grabbed it from Hadfield's toss, passed it back to another fan who, in turn, moved it further back in the audience.

By now it had become apparent that the crowd would

not cooperate and the mask made its way all the way up to the distant Blue (balcony) seats.

The fight eventually was broken up but Parent would not resume the game unless he had his mask returned. Garden public address announcer Pat Doyle pleaded with the fans to return the mask but it remained hidden and fans began chanting, "KEEP THE MASK! KEEP THE MASK!"

And they did. It never was returned; not the next day, the next year or the next decade.

As for Parent, he left the game to be replaced by Jacques Plante.

A few minutes later another fight erupted and, once again, Giacomin sped across the ice to join the fray. He jumped Plante, threw a headlock on him and pushed him against the boards. Fortunately, nobody relieved Jacques of his mask.

The Night of the Sobbing Goaltenders

Bill Durnan of the Montreal Canadiens won his first Vezina Trophy in 1944 and, according to his coach Dick Irvin, it was one of the worst things that ever happened to the Hall Of Fame goaltender. "From that time on," Irvin asserted, "Durnan became a man obsessed. Winning the Vezina became an obsession with him."

That obsession resulted in Durnan winning the goaltender's prize a total of six times, concluding with the 1949-50 season when an extraordinary event took place.

Durnan, although as great as ever, was getting on in years and the Canadiens owned a splendid youngster named Gerry McNeil, who played goal for their Montreal Royals farm team in the Quebec Senior Hockey League. If Durnan was ever injured, McNeil was on hand as a replacement.

One night, Durnan was involved in a serious accident which, Irwin believed, shortened his career. "A skate pierced his head," said Irvin, "and wrecked his nervous system. He cracked up after that."

Actually, McNeil replaced Durnan for only six games out of the 70 game schedule and turned in a magnificent 1.50 goals against average. Durnan's mark after 64 games was 2.20. Together they compiled a 2.14 average to win the Vezina.

"Durnan was so obsessed with the Vezina," said Irvin, "That if he had lost it that last year he played (1949-50), I think he would have been back playing goal the next year, bad nerves and all."

When the 1950 playoffs began, Durnan was in the Montreal net facing the New York Rangers. He played three games and allowed only ten goals for a 3.33 goals against average and, clearly, was not his championship self. As a result the Rangers, who had been underdogs, took a surprising lead in the series. Irvin, who was coaching Montreal at the time, decided to yank the veteran Durnan and gamble with the rookie McNeil.

"I'll never forget the night Durnan gave way to McNeil,"

Irvin recalled. "Gerry was as nervous as a kitten, so I thought if I got Bill to take him into another room and talk to him, the kid would quiet down."

Irvin made the suggestion and the two netminders — the grand, old man and the heir to the throne — disappeared into the anteroom. After a reasonable period of time Irvin expected them to come out so that McNeil could get on with the match, but neither was to be seen.

"Dick decided to investigate," a hockey writer remembered, "and went into the room. There he found his two goalies sitting together, crying!"

"Don't worry about a thing, Gerry. Everything is going to be alright."

In the other corner sat McNeil, author Ed Fitkin recalled: "Gerry said nothing; he was just sobbing." Irvin was dumbfounded — momentarily.

"I thought I pulled a boner," said Irvin, "but that night McNeil played one of the greatest games of his life!"

A Goalie's Illogical Logic

When Bernie Parent played goal for the Philadelphia Flyers, Bobby Hull was terrorizing netminders with a shot that often reached a speed of 100 miles per hour.

Harking back to those days, Parent now says, "Whenever Hull slapped one past me, I was happy."

Ron Low on Goaltending for an Expansion Team

(*Currently an assistant coach for the Edmonton Oilers, Ron Low guarded the nets for Washington in 1974-75 when the Capitals had one of the worst expansion teams in NHL annals.*)
One night," says Low, "we were losing something like 12-1 or 13-1 and I was looking for somewhere to hide. That's bad enough, right? What's worse, though, is that two of the goals were from guys on my own team.

Greg Joly wants to clear the puck and he puts it past me... top shelf. Jack Lynch puts in another one. What really turned me off, though, was that Lynch scores the only goal for us... and now he goes into the big dance, right? It's 12-0 against us, he scores a goal — and he's dancing!

"Bryan Watson, who played defense for us, skated over to Lynch and said, 'You ever do that again and I swear, I'll sucker you. I'll punch you out in front of all these people.' At that moment, Lynch stopped dancing."

The Goalie vs. Arnold Schwarzenegger

When goalie Clint Malarchuk was a rookie with the Quebec Nordiques, he decided to spend his post-season vacation with another goaltender, Brian Ford. The two single guys headed for Hawaii in search of women.

"We got on the beach," Malarchuk recalls, "and, all of a sudden, there were no girls. They were all gathered around Arnold Schwarzenegger... We were just standing there watching when, out of the blue, Brian kicks sand on Schwarzenegger.

"Next thing I knew, Ford took off, running, leaving me on my own. I remember Arnold looked at me, and I just hoped he'd think it was an accident.   And it wasn't even me who kicked the sand. I felt like the old Charles Atlas stuff of the bully kicking sand on the 90-pound weakling, only in reverse."

P.S. Schwarzenegger spared the goalie.

An Unbeatable Streak

In modern-day hockey, when NHL teams use two, three, four, or even five goalies in a season, it's hard to believe that just a few years ago teams relied on one man, and one man only, to guard their nets.

And no team relied on a single netminder more than

the Chicago Black Hawks in the sixties when Glenn Hall toiled for the Windy City Club. Game in and game out, Hall was always there. He played three, four, five hundred games in a row. Remember, this was in the era before the face mask, when all goaltenders suffered frequent cuts and concussions.

On the night of November 7th, 1962, Chicago was at home to Boston. And Hall wasn't feeling well. Of course, nobody expected him to feel well; his penchant for throwing up before games and in between periods was widely publicized. Similarly his habit of wrestling with the time trainer for several minutes in an effort to settle his pregame nerves had become a family ritual.

But on this night there was no wrestling in the dressing room. Hall's physical problems wouldn't allow it, for they were far worse than a nervous stomach. The pain in his lower back was excruciating. A lesser athlete wouldn't have thought of suiting up for the game. But when the Hawks took the ice that night, Hall was standing calmly between the pipes as usual. It was his 503rd consecutive game, or his 552nd counting the playoffs.

The game was only a few minutes old when Boston's Murray Oliver shot the puck at Hall and it flew right between his legs. Hall's back pain was so intense that he simply hadn't been able to bend over to block the puck the way he normally would have. It was impossible for him to carry on in goal.

Hall skated slowly to the Hawk bench, said a few words to his coach and then moved on to his dressing room, ending more than 33,000 consecutive minutes in his 503rd game of goaltending.

Say all you want about Lou Gehrig's consecutive game streak, but Glenn Hall's feat is the most impressive iron-man streak in professional sports history.

Best Putdown of a Silly Question

After his Penguins defeated the Rangers, 4-2, in the opening game of the Patrick Division finals in May 1992, Pittsburgh goalie Tom Barrasso was asked to appraise the work of his rival, John Vanbiesbrouck.

"I don't worry too much about the other end," said Barrasso. "I haven't had a goalie score on me yet."

Sawchuk's Dazzling Playoff

Ask any old-time hockey broadcaster to name the greatest goalie he's ever seen and chances are he'll tell you it's Terry Sawchuk. One of Sawchuk's remarkable records — 103 shutouts in a 20-year NHL career — may never be broken.

It was shutout goaltending that made Sawchuk famous back in 1952 when he was a second-year man with the Detroit Red Wings. In 1951, having captured the Calder Trophy as top rookie and having been named to the all-star team, he'd already established himself as one of the best goalies in the game. But nobody expected him to be almost flawless when the Wings met Toronto in the playoffs in 1952.

Sawchuk blanked the Leafs in the first two games 3-0 and 1-0, and allowed only three Toronto goals in the next two games (6-2 and 3-1 for Detroit). The Red Wings skated off with a four-game sweep of the semifinals.

The young goalie was just as hot against powerful Montreal when the final series opened at the Montreal Forum. Sawchuk gave up a single goal in game one and another lone score in game two. Both games went to Detroit, 3-1 and 2-1. Back on home ice, Sawchuk was even stingier. He chalked up two straight shutouts with identical 3-0 scores. Reporters agreed it was Sawchuk's brilliance that enabled the Red Wings to become the first team in history to sweep eight straight games en route to the Cup.

In the eight games, Sawchuk recorded four shutouts.

He gave up a mere five goals and his goals-against-average was an incredible 0.62. No playoff goalie has come close to matching that performance.

The Winnipeg native went on to other Cup triumphs — two more with the Red Wings in 1954 and 1955 and one with Toronto in 1967. But the Stanley Cup playoff that pleased him the most was the eight game sweep in the spring of '52.

Daryl Reaugh's Light-hearted Look at Goaltending

Daryl Reaugh was not a big-league goaltender for very long. He was up for the proverbial "cup of coffee" with Edmonton, understudying the great Grant Fuhr. In his professional maturity, he received another NHL chance with the Hartford Whalers. While he performed nobly, the club chose other puck stoppers and Reaugh spent the 1991-92 season with Springfield Indians of the American Hockey League.

Anyone who has met Reaugh, whether it be on the major or minor league level, is immediately struck by his ebullience and knack for finding humor in the difficult life of a hockey player. During the 1991-92 season Reaugh injured his knee and during his recuperation period took time out to chronicle some of his favorite stories for our Springfield reporter Audrey L. Nowak.

The interview room had a recliner and a couch. Audrey offered him the recliner which prompted Daryl to say he felt as if he was in a psychiatrist's office. To that, Nowak affected a German accent and asked, "Why do you hate your mother, and how has this contributed to your becoming a goaltender?" Reaugh laughed and shot back, "I had a rough childhood, doctor." From that point, the interview was off and running. The edited text follows.

I'll never forget my first training camp with Edmonton. I was 18 and the Oilers had just come off winning their first Stanley Cup and here I was with the same guys I had been idolizing as a kid. All of a sudden I was on the ice with them. The first day I spent most of the time watching *who* was shooting on me rather than *where* they were putting the puck.

At the end of the day the goalie coach came up to me and said, "Kid, you've got to learn how to relax." He knew that I was awestruck by the sight of Wayne Gretzky and Mark Messier and Glenn Anderson and that I was thinking I couldn't play against them. "Well," he said, "we'll just chop all their heads off and make them all the same type of player."

The next day I went out there and tried to follow his advice. Next thing you know Wayne Gretzky was coming at me. I was talking to myself, "Wow! It's Wayne Gretzky." Then, he scored on me and I said, "Geez, that was pretty good!"

It didn't matter who the shooter was as long as he was on the Cup team. Even their tough guy, Dave Semenko, did it. He got the puck and made a rush, and I just looked at him and muttered, "Jesus, Dave Semenko!" And he put one behind me. So, I was gone after three days of training camp. Back to Juniors you go, Daryl.

I finally made it to the Oilers and played about 120 minutes. It was incredible; I was there for sixty-some odd games and never played. I swear to God the fans must have been sitting there looking at me and saying, "Did he win the Lottery or something? How did he ever get there? I mean we pay for our tickets to watch every night and he gets to sit on the bench with the guys and watch every night."

With Grant Fuhr there, I figured I'd never play. On the afternoon of one game, I casually went over to the West Edmonton Mall to do some shopping. I knew I wasn't going to play because Grant was doing well. I got back to the hotel across from Northlands Coliseum at about three and figured I'd have a little nap. It was a Sunday six o'clock game but I didn't think I'd have trouble waking up. I was watching TV and thought I'd just nod off for a second and wake up so why put in a wake-up call with the hotel operator? Right away, I violated Rule Number One — Always Put In A Wake-Up Call.

Next thing I know the phone is ringing. It's our defenseman Jeff Beukeboom and he's calling from the Oilers' dressing room. "Razor," he says, "are you coming to the rink?" I really didn't know what was going on so, I said, "Yeah." He shot back, "Well, okay," and then hung up.

I didn't know it at the time but it was five after five and the team was going out on the ice at twenty-after — and I'm sleeping in my hotel room. Before I could move, the phone rang again. It was Beukaboom: "Razor, do you realize that it's a six o'clock game."

Boom! My heart just dropped. I ran over to the window and ripped open the curtains. The first thing I saw was the arena parking lot, almost full with people going to the game. "Oh, God!"

I ran to the closet and grabbed the new suit that I had bought; it still had the tags on it, and threw it on, ran across the street, through the arena, right into the dressing room, right into the back and took off my clothes.

I was just shitting that our coach and general manager, Glen Sather, would see me come in but somehow I got my gear on in time for the warm-up. When I went out on to the ice I was in an absolute fog. I couldn't believe what I had done. I mean, here I was twenty-three, with the Stanley Cup champions and I almost slept through a game.

After a while, I melded in with the champs. I began living with Kevin Lowe, the team's veteran defenseman who was very friendly with Gretzky. One New Year's Eve we went to a party; me, Kevin, Wayne and his wife-to-be, the actress Janet Jones. We were drinking some golden-colored champagne that looked like cheap house wine to me. I figured we could afford some good stuff so I said, "Wayne, why don't we get a bottle of Dom Perignon? I'll buy it."

Gretzky started smiling and I had no idea what was so funny. He said, "Razor, how much do you think Dom Perignon costs?" I told him I figured it was about $100 a bottle. He laughed, "Razor, you see these bottles. That's Krystelle that I bought. You know how much these cost? They go for $220 a bottle." And with that I shrunk down to size.

We were leaving the next day on a road trip, starting in Washington so when I got home I was ahead of Kevin. I took his alarm clock, put it in my room and set it for eight o'clock. Unfortunately, I must have had a bit too much champagne because I set the alarm for 8 p.m. instead of 8 a.m.

Morning came and no alarm went off but fortunately one of Kevin's pals had slept over and was going to drive us to the airport. Lowe was always prompt and when he realized what happened he was furious because he had never been late for anything in nine years of pro hockey. Well, we got to the airport, all disheveled, and all our teammates were there waiting on line.

Kevin didn't talk to me for two days. Finally, on the third day, he broke the ice and said, "Daryl, Rule Number One — Never take the alarm clock out of the nine-year veteran's room!"

I also roomed with rookies like myself and one of the most unusual was Beukeboom because of the way he ate. Jeff was a six-foot-five farm boy from Ontario who would eat everything in the house. Other players would have a pre-game meal. Beuk would come home from the morning day-of-game workout and have a little meal. He'd follow that with a pre-pre-game meal followed by a pre-game meal. Then he'd eat again about twenty minutes after he ate the pre-game meal. At that point he'd go to sleep for a bit, then awaken and have yet another meal before going to the rink.

After the game he'd come home and have *another* meal. I felt as if I was feeding a carburetor.

Another roommate of mine was Jim Ralph, a goalie like myself and a very proud guy. We were in the minors at the time and the club had three goalies — Warren Skorodenski being the third one — and Ralphie was the odd man out in the eyes of our coach Larry Kish. The only thing Kish would allow Ralphie do was stand on the ice — so he could get paid — but never get in the nets.

One day Ralphie was standing there on the ice for about twenty minutes and then, all of a sudden, he disappeared. Nobody knew what had happened to him until practice was over and we returned to the dressing room. There, strung up as if a goalie had actually hung himself, was all of Ralphie's goalie gear, mask and everything, along with a suicide note saying that Kish had driven him to kill himself. Needless to say, Ralphie never played another game after that with us.

Another time he was playing in Newmarket and this time really getting shelled. It was about 8-1 against him when he decided that's enough! After the eighth goal, he grabbed the net, turned it around and put it against the boards and just stood there in front of it. He said, "You're not getting another one on me!" The place went nuts.

Ralphie and I were roommates for a while and we were like a couple of high school girls, sitting up, gossiping and giggling all night long. He'd make me laugh and I'd make him laugh and it went on and on. Trouble was, our hotel had real thin walls and we'd be up giggling til five in the morning while our teammates next door would be banging on the wall, "Shut up you guys, shut up!"

Remember, we were the goalies and they had a way of getting even with us the next day in practice. They'd skate in and rip the puck high on us to teach us a lesson.

Getting even happens in a lot of ways, especially with guys who get too cocky. When I was playing in Halifax we had a guy like that named Donnie Biggs who was a pretty cocky fellow. The way that type of individual is handled usually comes by way of an old ritual prank; telling him he's being called up to the NHL.

In our case, the airport was about a 45-minute drive from Halifax and we worked out everything right down to getting the coaches in on it. To make the prank authentic we had a Telex sent to Biggs advising him he was being called up to Edmonton. His sticks were all taped together for the plane trip and he told his wife and was all excited. He grabbed his bags in the dressing room and went home to pack his suits and everything.

By this time the prank had gone so far that some of the younger guys were hesitating, "We can't let him drive all the way out there." But the older guys came back, "Oh, *yes* we can!"

They even went so far as to give him a special locater for his airline ticket when he got to the airport. Biggs said good-bye to his wife and drove all the way out to Halifax airport. When he got there, he went to the counter with his locater number. "Sorry, Mister Biggs," the lady said, "we don't have a ticket for you." He got excited and yelled, "But there's gotta be a ticket; I'm going to play in Edmonton."

Finally, somebody broke the news to him and he learned a little bit, I guess.

The young guys are often victims. There's a routine called The Shoeshine which is done at team meals. While the rest of the players are eating, one guy crawls under the table with a bowl of sour cream or one of the sauces and taps a little bit on each of the rookie's new dress shoes.

Then, the perpetrator, quick, gets back to his seat and taps on his glass. "Oh, what?" Someone else says, "Shoeshine!" And everyone pulls back from the table and the poor guy looks down and sees what happened to his oxfords.

I've seen this trick played on the same guy two or even three times in one meal because some of the fellows who do it — Kevin McClelland was one of the best — are amazing at the way they get under the table.

People say goalies are different and they are. We have

to be like politicians because if we get our teammates mad at us, they won't play for us. If a goalie is someone everyone hates, the players can screw him pretty easily so it's a good idea to be everyone's buddy.

As a backup goalie, you become like a priest and hear confessions from the guys all the time. Guys come back to the bench and ask questions like, "if I have that guy on the far side of me and he comes around..." and so on. These guys assume that I'm watching the game when my eyes may very well have drifted into the crowd. But I'll always tell them the right thing, "Oh, yeah, you did the right thing, sure. No that's not YOUR fault." And they feel good again. They just want to talk and be told that they did the right thing.

Goalies are a strange breed; they are different and, as a rule, the funniest guys on any team. It goes with the position because if you really took goaltending seriously all the time, you'd go nuts and never last. A lot of stuff is out of your control and there's nothing a goalie can do about it.

Ronnie Low taught me one of my best lessons when I was playing in Halifax. It was a 2-2 tie that went into overtime. A guy floated one in from outside the blue line; the puck hit my blocker went in and we lost.

I was in such a rush to get out of the building that I had my uniform off in record time and was out of the arena when fans were still leaving the place. When I got home, my pal, Jeff Beukeboom tried talking to me but I wouldn't have any part of it. Just then, Ron Low phoned and said, "Get over here!" I figured, "Oh, I'm in shit now. He's going to wring me."

So I went over to his place and he had a bottle of Grand Marnier and a bottle of rum and two dozen beers sitting there and his wife was cooking. He made me sit there and drink until most of it was gone and he said, "You know, you're going to have losses, you're going to have wins. You just can't take things to heart all the time. If you're going to do that, you won't last more than a couple of years in this game."

That told me I had to have a sense of humor through it all and I found that that makes life easier because you can't go through an 80-game season with a glum face.

When you're the back-up goalie the way I've been in many situations, you experience things people never know about. Like for the first ten or fifteen minutes of a game I'm on pins and needles because the other guy may not play well and then I've got to go in. After that I relax a bit. Sometimes, I wind up sitting next to a guy who isn't playing much or not at all and we become buddies and talk a lot. That guy is often called a "stopper."

As a young player it took me a long time to figure out what the hell they were talking about when they said a guy was a "stopper." Then, Kevin McClelland explained what it was: "I'm the guy who sits on the bench and I stop the defense from running into the forwards in the middle of the bench!"

The Goalie and the Gangsters

Hall of Famer Alex Connell rates as one of the all-time great goaltenders in the history of the National Hockey League. He holds the record for the longest shutout sequence, going six consecutive games without allowing a goal, an incredible feat he achieved in the 1927-28 season. He also shares the distinction, with Clint Bennedict, of playing goal on two Stanley Cup teams from two different cities. In 1926-27 Connell earned his first championship ring with the Ottawa Senators, and in 1934-35 he repeated with the Montreal Canadiens. Perhaps the most well known incident involving Connell occurred, however, when he came close to losing his life after getting involved with gangsters in New York City.

It was in 1932 at the old Madison Square Garden on Eighth Avenue and 50th Street in New York and the Americans were hosting the Detroit Falcons in a game that would decide whether or not the Americans would go into the playoffs later that spring. At the time they were owned by the infamous Bill Dwyer, reputed mob boss and undisputed King of the bootleggers in New York as well as several other states.

The game was tied at the end of regulation time 1-1, and the two teams went into a ten minute overtime period. With about five minutes left in the period, Detroit received a penalty, giving the Americans the much-needed manpower advantage. The New York players realized it was their opportunity to take the initiative and win the game. It was a must-win situation.

The red, blue and white clad Americans bore down and administered intense pressure on the Falcons and Connell, their goalie. Red Dutton, then a battling defenseman for New York, took a blistering shot that, according to the goal judge, eluded Connell and ricocheted in and — just as quickly — out of the net. The red light went on and the Americans celebrated their win. But trouble was brewing; the referee, George Mallinson, disallowed the goal. He claimed he had a perfect view of the play and the puck never went in. Connell agreed.

"The shot might have looked like a score to the goal judge but the rubber definitely did not enter my net," recalled the erstwhile goalie.

During the melee that ensued, the goal judge berated the shocked goalie with a string of the vilest profanities Connell had ever heard. Connell, being a man of dignity and pride, was not about to stand for any more of that kind of abuse. He skated around the back of the net and, taking advantage of the man's nose which was sticking through the mesh, bopped the goal judge directly and resoundingly on his protruding proboscis. This set the surprised and infuriated goal judge reeling in his own blood, and started a panic among the security force at the Gardens who knew the man to be a "high official in the Dwyer mob".

Alex Connell unknowingly put his life in great danger with one well-placed, ill-timed punch. But Connell was more concerned with the game, and after play was resumed (the goal was not not allowed) he held the Americans scoreless and the game ended deadlocked at 1.

As Alex Connell left the ice he noticed for the first time that there were policemen lining the walkway; everywhere he looked he saw the boys in blue in great force blocking the spectators from approaching the players. When he got in the dressing room and began peeling off his sweaty uniform, two plain-clothed detectives walked up, identified themselves to him, and then stood on either side of him with their guns drawn.

It was then that Connell realized the seriousness of the actions he had taken. It was explained to him that the man he had punched out was Dywer's right hand man, and that there might be some serious ramifications if proper precautions were not taken.

"Evidently," remembered Connell, "his fingers on the red light switch were as fast as his fingers on the trigger."

Quickly, after he had finished dressing, Connell was shuffled into a waiting taxi and driven, along with police escort, to the hotel where the team was staying. The cops combed the lobby for suspicious looking characters before bringing in the befuddled Alex Connell. He was then given strict instructions not to leave his room for the remainder of the evening, and that he would probably be quite safe if he followed these words of caution without question. Needless to say, Connell was willing to obey, his fear and anxiety mounting with every cloak and dagger maneuver by the detectives.

Connell recalls how the rest of the evening went: "An old friend was visiting me that night and after we had talked about the strange goings-on, we decided to leave the hotel and get sandwiches before I went to bed.

"We walked out the front door and had only walked about ten feet when I remembered the cop's warning.

Then I noticed there were some people standing around us, one big, mean looking guy came toward us. We ducked into a diner and seated ourselves at separate counters. The large man came in and ordered me to go over to him for questioning, adding that if I knew what was good for me I'd do what I was told.

"Then I walked over to him. He demanded, 'Aren't you Alex Connell, goalkeeper for the Detroit Falcons?' I replied that I not only did not know who Alex Connell was, but that I'd never heard of any Detroit Falcons.

"After a couple of minutes of him repeating the question and me repeating my answer, he apologized for bothering me and left."

When the cops heard about the incident from the hotel's night manager, they decided to stand guard outside Connell's room for the rest of the night.

The next day Connell learned that his quick thinking and fast talking had probably saved him from a one way ticket with the gun-slinging hoodlums.

"Years later a New York newspaper man told me that the police had established the fact that both of the gangsters I encountered that night had come to sudden endings. When I asked how, he said, 'Bang! Bang!'"

Chapter Two

ARRESTING CHARACTERS

Babe Pratt — Puck's Bad Boy

If having a good time was the standard by which we measure hockey ability, Babe Pratt would be the greatest hockey player of all time. As it was, Pratt was among the outstanding players of his day as one of the first offensive-defenseman on the ice, and a first-class mischief maker away from the rink.

Pratt was the leading scorer in all the leagues he played in, from midget to junior, before joining the New York Rangers. As a part of the Rangers 1940 Stanley Cup winners, Babe sacrificed individual scoring honors to fit in with what captain Art Coulter called "The Rangers Machine." In fact, whenever Pratt rushed over the blue line and tried to score on his own, his teammates would playfully rib him, saying, "For chrissakes, stay back and don't be messing up the forward lines!"

When World War II depleted the Rangers roster, Pratt was sent to the Toronto Maple Leafs for two warm bodies. Coach Hap Day gave Pratt the green light to stickhandle when and where he pleased and Babe responded to his emancipation by winning the Hart Trophy as the league's most valuable player in 1944. Babe ended his playing career in the NHL with the Boston Bruins after suffering a painful knee injury, but he later returned to hockey as the good will ambassador of the Vancouver Canucks, and became the favorite speaking guest of hockey playing youngsters all over Western Canada, before his death.

There was a time in Pratt's career when parents may have questioned the influence of the fun-loving defenseman on their children. Former Ranger General Manager Lester Patrick certainly would have had misgivings, for it was the legendary Patrick who dubbed Pratt "Puck's Bad Boy."

"It seemed like every time Lester walked into a room," Pratt recalls, "especially during the playoffs, I wouldn't necessarily be drinking, but I would be there. I always got caught. Somebody else could be drinking away in another hotel or pub, but Lester always managed to find me. It seemed to me at the time that I wasn't doing any harm, but Lester used to make it a lot worse than it was and I used to go along with it as a gag. A couple of times he chastised me, and he caught me on more serious things. One time, he said, 'I'm not going to fine you, I'm not going to trade you, I'm going to send you to the minors until you rot.'"

Pratt laughed because he was sure Lester would never go through with his threat, knowing that Pratt could play for any team in the league. "He finally wound up fining me $1,000, a fantastic sum when you're making only $5,000 for the year. He kept it for one month, but I was playing so well that he felt guilty and gave it back."

That wasn't the only time Patrick tried to change Pratt's evil ways by imposing a stiff fine on his star blue-liner. When Babe reported to training camp in September 1940, he was full of ginger, and he didn't slow down as the Rangers embarked on their usual exhibition tour. One night he checked into the team's Pullman car at 3 A.M., only to discover that Lester was waiting up for him. "Babe," said Patrick, "I'm fining you $1,000. But if you don't take another drink for the rest of the campaign, I'll refund your money at the end of the season."

Pratt went on the wagon and the Rangers went on a long, long, losing streak. Patrick was worried and, one day, suggested to Babe that maybe a drink wouldn't hurt at all. "No, no," said Pratt, "my word is my bond."

Word of the Patrick-Pratt meeting leaked to the players. They figured that if the Babe didn't get off the wagon the club would really be in trouble. They told Pratt they would chip in and raise $1,000, if only he would have an occasional drink or two. But Pratt was adamant. The Rangers wound up in fourth place and were knocked right out of the playoffs by Detroit. "There's a moral to that story," Pratt said years later, "but I've been trying for thirty years and still haven't been able to figure it out."

Babe and Lester didn't always get along, especially when money was the subject. According to Pratt, Patrick wasn't tight with money, "he was adjacent to it!" Lester finally traded Babe to Toronto in 1942, and to Pratt's astonishment he was paid more by the Leafs than Lester ever paid him. As a result, he began to play even better. When Lester heard about Pratt's good fortune, he asked Babe about it.

"Lester," Pratt explained, "now I'm being paid enough to eat on. I'm finally getting the wrinkles out of my belly."

Occasionally, old Rangers would get together in the minors, where many of them settled into coaching jobs. Bun Cook was one of them. He ended up in Cleveland, coaching Jim Hendy's Barons of the American League at a time when Babe was skating out his career with the Hershey Bears.

Once, Cleveland was demolishing Pratt's Hershey Sextet, 9-0. Late in the game, Babe, who was well on in his hockey years, skated past the Barons bench. His old pal, Cook, looked up at the scoreboard and shouted down to Pratt, "It's 9-0, Babe. what are you going to do about it?"

"Nothing to it," Babe shot back. "A touchdown and a field goal."

The Maple Leafs thought they had the solution to calming Pratt's wild and wily nature when Babe was still in his prime in Toronto. It was decided that Hap Day could keep Pratt on the straight and narrow only if his star player was close by at all times. So Day and Pratt became roommates. "It was the worst time of my life," Pratt said of the sleeping arrangement, "because we were awake until four in the morning while he talked hockey. I'd scream at him, 'Jesus, I could be out drinking and here we are talking about hockey!' That used to make him mad and he'd say, 'If you had laid off that stuff you'd have been the greatest hockey player who ever lived.' Every time I've ever had to call him in later years he'd say, 'Hello' and I'd say, 'This is the greatest,' and he knows who it is immediately."

Pratt readily admits that Day was the "greatest coach in hockey," but he didn't have too much fun when Hap was around. "He wasn't a very complimentary guy," Babe recalls. "If you bumped into him in the street, he'd say 'Nice pass you made in Chicago' and that would mean that you gave the puck away.

"I'll always remember the final game in Detroit when we won the Stanley Cup (in 1945) and I scored the winning goal. Before the game started, Hap paced around the living room of the suite while I was snoring in bed. He came in and dumped me right out of bed and yelled, "How the hell can you lay there and snore before the seventh game of the Stanley Cup Finals?" I said, "Well, the game doesn't start for another hour. There's no use me doing any worrying until then; that's your job.'"

Pratt was just as colorful when talking about today's hockey, which he believed was more exciting than his era because of the bigger, faster players in the NHL these days. That, however, didn't mean he wasn't without criticism of the current game.

"The whole concept of coaching today is to stop the good players from playing better," Pratt said. "Very seldom do you see the best player in Toronto playing against the best player in Montreal. Guys like Scotty Bowman have their defensive units playing against the players giving them the most trouble. In the old days you used to pit the so-called big line against the opposing big line and let the chips fall where they may. I always say they cook the goose that laid the golden egg. When people paid money to see Babe Ruth play, they didn't pay to see him walked."

Pratt would ramble on about his rollicking days as a player and the current state of hockey at the dozens of functions he was invited to each year. "I've been to 107 towns and hamlets in British Columbia," he said, "and some of the places I've been back to 10-12 times. I talk at their luncheons, dinners, stag parties, and, of course, I'm also invited to minor hockey dinners. I'm the perennial guest of a peewee tournament they've had in Vernon, B.C. for nine years."

For Babe, the most fun came from meeting the youngsters as he travelled from town to town. "Of course I enjoy meeting the kids on the street and in the rinks, talking to them and kidding them. They'll say, 'My number is 15 and you watch me play. I'll show you something!' I'll see the kid afterward and say, 'You're number 15, you were terrible.' The kid will get flustered defending himself and we'll joke around and have a great time."

Having a great time, after all, was as much Babe Pratt's profession as was playing hockey.

The Devils Talk About Their Resident Humourist Ken Daneyko

Doug Brown: Ever since I joined the club in the late 1980's Kenny was the one who had the best one-liners. The line I best remember took place on the final night of the season in 1987-88 when we beat the Blackhawks in Chicago to clinch our first playoff berth.

Dano, who very rarely scored a goal, got one early in the game and we were all celebrating. Kenny skated over to the bench and said to the guys, "Get me off the ice! I'm too excited to play!!"

Eric Weinrich: "One night Kenny got a roughing penalty. As the ref announced it to the penalty timekeeper, Dano skated over and said, "Man that wasn't a penalty, that was pure POWER!"

Bearcat on the Prowl

Jim ("Bearcat") Murray, the very bald, lovable Calgary Flames trainer, is one of the most unusual characters in hockey for one very good reason; he dons a pair of rollerblades at every rink he visits and madly skates around the aisles until he works himself into exhaustion.

Murray is beloved for other reasons, not the least of which is his sense of humour and upbeat personality. During a visit to New York's Madison Square Garden, Bearcat agreed to an interview about hockey flakes, himself included.

Q. Why do you roller skate around arenas while your team practices?

Bearcat: First, for exercise and second because it's awfully boring just sitting around watching a scrimmage. It gives me something to do. I've done it for ten years and the only problem is that in some arenas the rows are narrow, so it gets pretty dangerous. I've got to sidestep lots of leftover cups and crap like that.

Q: When you think of a funny hockey player, who comes to mind?

Bearcat: Doug Gilmour of the Leafs. When he played for us, he was quite a practical joker. One of his routines was to bring in a box of donuts for the whole team; which was nice until you realized that he had dipped them in wax. Sometimes, he'd buy jelly donuts but he'd manage to insert shaving cream where the jelly was supposed to be. When he still was playing, Lanny McDonald was quite a prankster. He liked to hide in teammate's closets or under the bed and then scare the hell out of his roommate.

Another standard was short-sheeting the beds in the hotel, putting shaving cream between the folded towels and sewing socks together. Or taking a player's car out of the arena parking lot while he's practicing and moving it out of sight. When he finishes practice, he figures it got stolen.

Q. What was your most embarrassing moment in the NHL?

Bearcat: It happened during the 1989 playoffs between the Flames and the Kings and, basically, I wound up going out on the ice while play was still in progress; although I didn't know it at the time. What happened was that Bernie Nicholls of the Kings had hit our goaltender and he went down and immediately a fight broke out.

Now everybody who follows hockey knows that when a fight starts, play stops. At least that's what I figured this time and, besides, my natural instinct was to run out to aid my injured goalie.

Well, whaddya know; play hadn't stopped and here I am running out on the ice while the play is heading in the other direction and a goal was actually scored with me out there. It was a case of me thinking I had heard a whistle when actually I had heard nothing of the kind. Talk about embarrassing; that was it!

Q. You were trainer for Calgary's Cup-winning team. We've heard a lot of stories about what happened to the Stanley Cup after it was won so there must be a good one about the Flames.

Bearcat: There sure is a good one. When we flew home from Montreal — where we won The Cup — to Calgary, the Cup was turned over to one of our owners, Darryl Seaman, and he took it out to his horse farm.

All of the cowboys and ranch workers were thrilled to see the Cup and wanted to have their pictures taken with it. As far as I know, this could have been the first time The Stanley Cup was brought to a horse farm but I'll bet there was a first in another way. One of the horses was supposed to be fed some hay and one of the cowboys simply stuffed the hay into the Cup and the horse had his dinner right out of The Stanley Cup. Not many horses can make that statement.

Q. What was the best sight-gag you ever saw pulled off by a hockey player?

Bearcat: We were on a flight from New York City to Calgary. On this particular plane half the team was put in the first-class section while the rest of the players were back in economy with other regular passengers.

Lanny McDonald was one of the lucky guys in first-class and after we were airborne, he got up from his seat, went to the washroom and changed his clothes. Of course, nobody was then paying attention to him.

Next thing you knew, he walked out of the washroom wearing a bathing suit with a towel wrapped around his neck. He pulled open the curtain separating first-class from the economy section so that everyone could see him in his bathing trunks.

Before anyone could utter a word, Lanny announced to the entire economy group, "COME ON UP, GUYS, THE POOL'S GREAT; HEATED AND ALL!"

Was Mike Walton Hockey's Craziest Player?

One of the endless debates among puck savants concerns the important topic: who is the prize, all-time hockey cashew?

Nuts have populated the ice game from the day the first puck was dropped and there certainly are no statistics one can produce to ascertain that King Clancy was crazier than Eddie Shack or that Tiger Williams had it over Turk Sanderson.

So when it comes to dipsy skaters one's subjectivity comes to the fore as in the case of author Michael Farber. The way the Montreal Gazette columnist sees it, there is no contest.

"Mike Walton was the craziest player in hockey," says Farber. Period. No arguments, please. "Eddie Shack took a hockey schtick and beat people over the head with it and Derek Sanderson was first-team crazy in the lifestyle-abuse category, but Shaky Walton was the biggest nut in the bowl."

Walton also was a pretty fair hockey player with the Toronto Maple Leafs who later cashed in on the big-money policies of the World Hockey Association in the mid-1970s. He was a compact skater with a big smile and a ready quip.

During an interview with Farber, Walton confessed that the craziest thing he ever did took place when he played for the WHA's Minnesota Fighting Saints.

"We were in the playoffs against Gordie Howe and his sons (Marty and Mark) who were playing for Houston," said Walton. "They were eliminating us and I was mad. With a couple of minutes left, I had the attendant pull the car next to the dressing room. I took off while the game was going on, wearing my uniform and skates with the skateguards, and drove to downtown Minneapolis to a bar. I sat there in my uniform and my skates having a few drinks. Then I left."

Farber wouldn't argue that that was *the* craziest thing Walton had ever done but he has a pretty fair alternate.

"Once Shaky forgot how heavy hockey equipment can be and jumped into a swimming pool in his uniform after a practice.

Walton was among several Maple Leaf players who won Stanley Cups under the dictatorial George ("Punch") Imlach in the early 1960's. Imlach was a smart man until it came to player relations, a subject in which he regularly failed. Punch was so harsh with superstar Frank Mahovlich — Imlach deliberately mispronounced his name Ma-hal-o-vich — that the Big M nearly suffered a nervous break-down.

Imlach was no less gentle with Walton who got fed up more times than he can count. "Once," Walton remembered, "I was so upset I got off a moving train. It was coming to Montreal. I was upset so I retired. I retired three or four times. We'd leave Toronto at Midnight, and I told Bob Pulford who was our captain, to tell Punch I was leaving. The train started, and I hopped off."

Walton was one of hockey's early rebels and demonstrated his revolutionary tendencies by breaking Imlach's neatness code. Imlach preferred brush cuts and short hair. Shaky came to camp one year with extra long locks worthy of Little Orphan Annie. But the coach got even. He hired a couple of musclemen who doubled as Leafs trainers and told them where Walton was sleeping. The rest is tonsorial history.

Armed with a pair of scissors, the trainers slipped into Mike's room and, while one pinned him to the bedsheets, the other snipped off the Walton locks.

For a while, it appeared that Imlach had won the battle, but Farber noted otherwise: "Walton wrenched his back getting the trim and missed some games. So while Imlach paced the bench in his fedora, Walton sat in the stands behind him wearing a Beatles wig!"

The Unspeakable Cowboy Flett

Bill ("Cowboy") Flett is regarded as the first eccentric to play for the early 1970's Philadelphia Flyers, a.k.a. the Broad Street Bullies.

"Bill," said Philadelphia broadcaster Gene Hart, "looked the part, with his long sideburns, his black beard, and a long feather in his ten-gallon hat.

Before coming to Philadelphia, Flett played for the Los Angeles Kings which then were owned by transplanted Canadian multi-millionaire Jack Kent Cooke.

When Flett was dealt to the Flyers, Cooke had been persuaded that The Cowboy would do little damage as a scorer but when Philly met the Kings on Flett's first return to Cooke's fabulous Forum, he learned differently.

Trailing 3-2 in the third period, the Flyers rallied to win on Flett's natural hat trick (three straight goals). Earlier in the game, Cowboy had set up another Flyer goal which meant he had four points and thus qualified to be named first star of the game.

However, Flett was not even named third star; he was completely overlooked by the selector. However, Hart, in his autobiography, SCORE! revealed the reason why: "The reason for his being 'overlooked' was that Cooke had been so upset by his former employee's performance, that he charged down to inform the off-ice officials. You do not announce Bill Flett. Announce him and I'll fire you!'

"In the dressing room after the game, Bobby Clarke presented Flett with a spittoon for his performance as 'unspeakable star of the game.'"

Cowboy Flett Exposes Bobby Clarke

When Clarkie and I played for the Philadelphia Flyers in the mid-1970s, he was a terrific captain, and leader. But what few people realize is that he also was something of a practical joker.

One of his favorite things while sitting at a bar was taking his false teeth out of his mouth and dropping them in somebody's drink.

Clarkie and I were roommates when this happened. We were sitting at a bar and, right on schedule, he takes his teeth out and plunks them right into my glass.

He must have turned away for a second because I got them out before he noticed and hid them til we got out of the bar and then managed to plant them in his suitcase.

For ten days he looked high and low for them while we were on the road but he couldn't for the life of him find his molars. Finally, when he returned home to Philadelphia, he unpacked his valise and, there they were!

The Great Gabbo

Eddie Dorohoy, who played for the Montreal Canadiens in post World War II years, could probably be called the most outspoken player to hit the big time. Unfortunately, his gift for gab was greater than his hockey ability.

Dorohoy received his basic training for the National Hockey League in Lethbridge, Alberta where he played for a junior team known as the Native Sons. It was there that Dorohoy's vociferousness and his unorthodox behavior on ice became famous or perhaps infamous throughout Western Canada.

Even when Dorohoy blinked his eyes he seemed to do it in a flamboyant way, and when he took the ice you knew he was there. "He played centre," said Herb Goren, the former New York Rangers' publicist, "like Connie Mack used to manage his baseball club. He used his stick for directional signals before every face off, the way Mack waved his scorecard."

Dorohoy was only nineteen years old when the Montreal Canadiens promoted him to the NHL. Normally a rookie would be awed in the hallowed surroundings of the Canadiens dressing room, with immortals such as Maurice "Rocket" Richard and Elmer Lach around him. But not Eddie "The Pistol" Dorohoy.

The moment coach Dick Irvin placed the rookie on a line with Lach and Richard, Dorohoy began telling the old masters how the game should be played. On one occasion the three of them were launching a rush during an inter-squad scrimmage when Dorohoy abruptly skidded to a halt and demanded a conference. It was like Jimmy Durante telling the New York Philharmonic to "Stop the Music!" in the middle of Beethoven's Fifth.

Dorohoy somberly called Richard and Lach over to him. "Listen," he said, glaring at the pair as if he was the coach, "the trouble with you guys is that you're out of position."

Irvin, who was watching the episode from the sidelines, nearly fell over backward with laughter at the sight of Dorohoy lecturing his stars. But Dorohoy noticed Irvin out of the corner of his eye and demanded that the coach cease and desist immediately. "What's so funny," said Dorohoy, reprimanding the senior coach in the league. "Richard and Lach can make mistakes, too. I'm only trying to help them."

Dorohoy wasn't much help to the Canadiens that season. They slumped terribly and Irvin soon became disenchanted with him. Dick suggested that the 150 pound Dorohoy go on a crash diet to increase his weight on the theory that it would help his scoring potential. Eddie managed to stuff himself enough that he finally reached 162 pounds.

"Now," said Irvin, "you're too fat and soft!" "The only thing soft," countered Eddie, "is your head."

"Maybe," snapped his coach, "but you're benched."

Even with Dorohoy on the sidelines the Canadiens lost. Irvin was beside himself with rage and wished that he could persuade his gabby forward to learn how to score goals. "Why can't you put the puck in the net?" demanded the exasperated Irvin.

"From the angle on the bench I'm sitting on," quipped Dorohoy with unimpeachable logic, "I'm lucky to touch the puck."

That did it as far as Irvin was concerned. He demoted Dorohoy to the Canadiens' farm club in Dallas, Texas, which was about as far away from Montreal as Irvin could send a player, although Dick thought he could still hear Dorohoy's voice echoing clear across the United States. "Sure, I pop off," Dorohoy agreed, "but I don't say anything malicious. What's the use of living if you can't say what you think?"

Dorohoy eventually wound up playing for Victoria in the Western Hockey League, and if anything, his filibustering increased. "I must be the only hockey player in history," he boasted, "who was ever fined in the summer. Hell, I just took it out of my unemployment insurance."

By the time Eddie was twenty-two years old he had been named the coach of the Victoria sextet. That made him one of the youngest coaches of a professional team in any sport and he was favorably compared to baseball's boy managers Lou Bordreau and Bucky Harris. Unfortunately, the Pistol never enjoyed the same success as his baseball counterparts. Needless to say, it wasn't Dorohoy's fault, and anyone who didn't believe it could quickly find out by asking him. "It was just that I had a bad club." Eddie would explain. "The only thing that improved was my misconduct record."

Dorohoy played for four consecutive years in Victoria and managed to stay among the top three scorers in each of those seasons. By the mid-fifties the New York Rangers were expressing interest in the young man, and Ranger manager Frank Boucher requested and received permission to invite the Pistol to the New York training camp.

"There were a lot of interesting characters in that camp," recalled Herb Goren. "There was goalie Gump Worsley, and that rugged individualist Lou Fontinato, but for sheer force of personality Dorohoy was easily the 'best of show'".

Wren Blair — Laughs with a Loser

Coaching a losing team can be a dreadful experience; one that frays the nerves, increases aspirin intake and inspires eccentric behavior. Nobody knows this better than Wren Blair who coached the Minnesota North Stars a quarter century ago when they were one of the NHL's brand-new expansion teams.

Starting in 1967-68 the NHL ballooned from six to twelve teams. The Original Six were the established clubs like the Montreal Canadiens and the Toronto Maple Leafs while the expansion clubs included the North Stars, Philadelphia Flyers and St.Louis Blues, among others.

The newcomers were stripped bare of talent which

meant that a lot of improvising was necessary, especially behind the bench. Blair, who had come to the North Stars after considerable pro hockey experience, never missed a trick to get his club on track.

"One night we were in St.Louis," said Blair, "and I tried every motivational tool short of getting out a shotgun and we're only down 2-1 after the second period. So I went into the dressing room and wandered around there for a while. I'm ranting and raving and I realize nobody is even listening. So I say, 'All right, if you're not gonna even listen, let me tell you guys something. I noticed some guys in the stands, with big glasses of beer, their feet up, enjoying themselves. I'm gonna go up there with 'em. The hell with you guys. I'm quitting on you.' And I stalked out."

The North Stars then proceeded to win the hockey game.

Minnesota Star Tribune columnist Dan Barreiro recalled another time when the North Stars were playing the Los Angeles Kings. In the first period Minnesota defenseman Mike McMahon made a "horrible pass" thus enabling the Kings to score.

"We came into the dressing room," said Blair, "and I take off my topcoat and try throwing it at McMahon. Well, you know the guys would eat oranges and there were some orange peels on the floor. So when I throw the topcoat toward McMahon, I go right with it. Go straight in the air and fall on my back onto the floor. But I keep yapping and yelling even when I'm flat on my back.

"So I get up and see this garbage can and kick it straight into the air, and garbage goes flying all over the room. My trainer walked in when I was on the floor. The next day, we're on a plane and he says, 'Lemme ask you something. What the hell kind of play were you trying to demonstrate when you were on the floor?'"

The art of demonstration was developed to a science by Blair. One of his better players in those early years was a slick forward named Parker MacDonald. But even an ace can err and MacDonald gave the puck away in the North

Stars' zone and nearly hurt the club. Looking at MacDonald on the bench, Blair said, "Parker, that play will cost you one hundred dollars."

When MacDonald protested, Blair threatened to double the fine. After the period ended, Blair herded his players to the dressing room. "I started thinking I could really get some mileage out of this with the younger players," he remembered. "I could really get their attention that I meant business. So I went up to Parker and I said, 'I changed my mind on that $100'. And he looked at me as if to say, 'I figured you would. Who the hell else you got on this team?' And I said, 'Instead you report to Memphis tomorrow.' And he said, 'Memphis?' I said, 'Yeah, Memphis. It's our farm club in the deep South.'"

Utter futility seemed to bring out the best in Blair. There was a one-sided game in Pittsburgh that found the North Stars trailing 8-1 at the end of the second period.

"I had pretty much used every verb and adjective I know getting on them from the bench. So I went in and stomped around a little, but there was no chance. This wasn't a 2-1 situation like in St.Louis. So I went into a little room next to the locker room and just sat there all by myself. This was the kind of door you could lock from the outside with a padlock.

"Well, while I was in there by myself somebody throws the padlock on and locks the door. So the buzzer goes off to start the third period, and I can't get out. I hear them yelling and hollering on their way out to the ice, like they're all excited. I'm locked in. So I say, 'To hell with these SOBs. I'm not gonna say a word. I'll get out of here sooner or later.' That's where I stayed for the whole last period. Eventually my trainer let me out, but I never let those guys know I was mad."

Barreiro resurrected a wonderful Blair tale about the time he attended an NHL softball game in Niagara Falls which featured several of his players from the early expansion era. Until that time Blair had never let on how angry he had been on that night in Pittsburgh.

Blair: "A bunch of the guys from that team were talking to me, and they were saying, 'Boy, it must've been frustrating to be a coach with a bunch of guys like us.' I said, 'Oh, yeah.' And they said, 'If anybody ever did something like lock a coach in the dressing room, boy, I bet that would've been pretty irritating.'

"And I said, 'Is that what you guys have been thinking all these years? Hey, lemme tell you something. I was so damnned delighted I didn't have to watch you imbeciles on the ice for another period, I didn't mind being locked in there at all.'"

A Booming Cast

Hall of Famer Bernie ("Boom Boom") Geoffrion was a Jekyll-Hyde type when he played for the Montreal Canadiens. At once he was a serious performer and team clown. During the 1960-61 season, the serious side of Boomer emerged after he suffered a badly injured knee shortly before the playoffs.

The Canadiens had won an unprecedented five straight Stanley Cups prior to the 1961 playoffs and Geoffrion was determined to play although he was wearing a cast on the knee.

As the Habs entrained for Chicago and the opening round series against the Black Hawks, Geoffrion decided to take medical matters into his own hands.

"I felt the cast was starting to come loose and wanted to get it off," Boomer recalled. "I figured that I could do that and they could shoot my injured knee up with cortisone and I could play, even if it was just on the power play.

"So I got our defenseman Doug Harvey and said, 'Doug, why don't you get a knife and cut the damned thing.' He agreed and we went into the Ladies Room and with a small pocketknife it took Harvey five hours to cut the cast off. Boy, you should have seen the Ladies Room after we finished with all the little pieces of the cast everywhere.

"Anyway, I went to bed and the next morning when I started to walk the pain was unbelievable. It hurt so much but I didn't say anything because I wanted to play even though no one was going to force me.

"I went to (coach) Toe Blake and the trainer and told them and they really got mad and gave me hell. They wanted to know how I was going to do it. I told them just freeze the knee and I'd be OK. So, they let me do it and I played.

"I remember the first shift because Bobby Hull and Reggie Fleming knew about the injury but they didn't want to hurt me badly. Still, they were taking a crack at it and hitting me pretty good. I don't know whether it was worth the try but after the game, when the shots wore off, God, I couldn't even walk."

Hound Kelly's Logic
When Bob ("Hound") Kelly — also known as Muttley — played for the Philadelphia Flyers 1974 and 1975 Stanley Cup champions, he frequently was teased about his I.Q.

Broadcaster Gene Hart once said that The Hound was "so dumb that his was the only name on the Stanley Cup that was written in crayon — the name Muttley, that is."

A favorite Flyers-Kelly story was about the time Hound was rooming in an apartment building with defenseman Wayne Hillman.

It was a Sunday morning and Kelly had returned from church in a rainstorm. When he arrived in the apartment he admonished Hillman. "You call me dumb, but it's raining and your car is outside with the windows open."

Hillman properly wondered, "Why didn't you close the windows?"

To which Kelly deadpanned: "I couldn't; the doors were locked!"

Hall of Famer Bill Gadsby's Most Arresting Personalities

Bill Gadsby was one of the rare individuals who starred in the NHL for two decades. He broke in with the Chicago Black Hawks after World War II and later starred for the New York Rangers and Detroit Red Wings. Despite his lengthy career, Gadsby never had the good fortune to play for a Stanley Cup-winner.

Detroit-based reporter Jim Ramsey encountered Gadsby one day at Joe Louis Arena and coaxed a few stories out of him about the most arresting personalities Bill encountered during his super career.

Today you call them "Flakes" but when I was playing in the National Hockey League we referred to them as "Ding Dongs."

Believe me, there were quite a few back when we had a six-team league in the pre-expansion era. Two of the most memorable were Eddie Shack and Larry Zeidel.

Larry and I were teammates for a while on the Chicago Black Hawks and, let me tell you, there was never a more intense guy on the ice. Zeidel was fierce. Once, when he was playing defense for Edmonton, he and a tough defenseman named Jack Evans, who was with Saskatoon, got into an unbelievably vicious stick fight. They actually broke the sticks over each others heads and then fought with the broken ends until they were a bloody mess.

Zeidel would do anything to get himself up for a game including the playing of John Phillip Sousa marches the afternoon of a night game.

Shack and I were teammates on the Rangers. Eddie had a big nose and had a strong physique. He liked to fool around a lot but he also got into a lot of trouble on the ice because he was always charging people.

When I was with the Rangers we had an exhibition game in a small city in Ontario and Zeidel's team, now in the American League, was on the other side.

All of a sudden, during the first period, Shack and

Zeidel started high sticking each other. Let me tell you it was mean. Real MEAN! They swung so hard they broke their sticks over each other's shoulders. Then they started spearing each other in the belly with the broken shafts.

Of course, both of them were kicked out of the game.

When the period ended, we returned to our dressing room and, by now, Shack was showered and all dressed. I asked him what he planned to do and he said he was going to watch the rest of the game.

My advice to him was that he had better watch himself. I figured Zeidel was crazy and liable to come after him again off the ice but Eddie said he didn't want any more to do with Larry and was just going to sit in the stands behind our bench.

The second period started and everything was normal until I heard a commotion behind our bench. Sure enough, Zeidel had spotted Shack sitting in the stands, came down and jumped Eddie and they began swinging away again. It got so bad that the police were called in and, incredibly, they started fighting with the cops!

Well, it got so bad, we emptied our benches and started helping out. When the dust had cleared, Shack and Zeidel were taken down to the police station.

Shack had a bit of talent but he used to drive the Rangers coach, Phil Watson, crazy with his antics. I should point out that Watson was a wild and emotional coach in his own right and could be very tough on his players.

There was this night when Watson came into the dressing room after we had played a poor first period. Phil took off on everyone, player by player, really letting the guys have it over what they had done wrong.

By the time he got to Shack you could hear Watson's voice all the way across town. "SHACK, YOU'RE LOAF-ING, YOU'RE NOT HITTING AND YOU'RE NOT PLAY-ING DEFENSE. DO YOU UNDERSTAND WHAT I'M TELLING YOU?"

Eddie looked up and put both his index fingers in his

ears and moved them in and out letting Watson know it was going in one ear and out the other.

The dressing room broke up with laughter. We were still laughing like crazy as we headed out to the ice for the next period.

Then, I looked over at Watson. He was actually crying.

Zeidel produced a few laughs, himself, when we were together in Chicago. There was this road trip — in those days we travelled almost exclusively by train — to Montreal and we all were sitting in the club car relaxing when the conductor come through.

He told everyone that at the next stop, the club car would be uncoupled from the train and hooked on to another train that was heading for Ottawa in a different direction from where we were going. "Whoever is going to Montreal," he said, "should return to his own car."

A bunch of us got up and returned to our Pullman and when the train pulled in to the next stop, the trains uncoupled and we then continued on to our destination, Montreal.

As we were picking up speed, leaving the station, we passed another train on the track across from us. Like ourselves, that train had just started to move and was slowly accelerating but still going slow enough for us to see right into their coaches.

I looked over and did a double-take. Sitting there in that train's club car was none other than my teammate, Zeidel, heading for Ottawa!

Everyone started yelling and banging on the windows trying to get Larry's attention, but of course he couldn't hear us. When Zeidel got to Ottawa and realized how he had blundered, he had to charter a plane to get him to Montreal on time for the game. It cost him a young fortune at a time when we weren't making much in the NHL. The mistake damn near killed Larry because he was tight with his money.

Gordie Howe was a teammate of mine on the Red Wings for several years but my first major encounter with him, oddly enough, happened while I was in my last day with the Rangers.

I had known the great Howe as an opponent for a long time. I remember when he destroyed Lou Fontinato, then the Rangers tough guy defenseman, in a fight at Madison Square Garden and I saw Howe score many a pretty goal.

One night we were home at Madison Square Garden for a game against the Red Wings. It was a time when there had been a lot of rumors that our general manager Muzz Patrick was going to make a big trade. For weeks no trade happened and now we were in another game. At one point the puck went into the corner and Howe and I wound up going after it. I gave Gordie a pretty good going over and he turned around and said, "Take it easy, Gads, we're going to be teammates after this game."

I said, "What the hell are you talking about?"

Gordie said, "You're going to be traded to Detroit right after the game."

I figured it was a trick of his to take my mind off the game.

Shortly after the game, Patrick stopped me and said that I had been traded to the Red Wings. I never did tell him that Howe had already told me about it during the game.

When I got to Detroit, Gordie and I met for coffee at a local restaurant. He wanted to fill me in on my new teammates as well as management. The boss of the Red Wings at the time was old Jack Adams, who had been the coach and later general manager of the club and was one of the most famous executives in the game. He also was one of the most emotional characters.

"Listen," said Howe, "I've got to tell you something about Jack Adams. We keep a table full of oranges in the middle of the dressing room to eat and suck on between periods.

"If you ever see Adams come in and puck up one of those oranges and take a big bite out of it, don't take your eyes off him. What he'll do is start turning around and then throw it! He never knows where it's going, so watch him."

Sure enough, in the next game, we came in after the first period and there's Jack. He walks over to the crate and picks up an orange, takes a big bite, starts to turn and hauls off and throws it. The orange landed half way up a wall and splattered all over the place.

From that time on, I never took my eyes off Jack Adams.

Another important character I got to know was Maurice Richard, The Rocket. When I played against him, which was until he retired after the 1959-60 season, it was hard to know Rocket because he was such an intense competitor. He hated the opposition with a passion you wouldn't believe.

I got to understand that passion when I met Richard ten years after I retired.

The Canadiens were going to Europe to play some games against the Armed Forces teams but a couple of their players couldn't make it so I was invited to come along with Jimmy Peters.

We were on a train, travelling to play a game and Jimmy and I had been in the club car for quite a while. I got tired and told Peters I was going to my room to go to sleep.

A few minutes later there was a knock on the door. It was Peters. "The Rocket wants to talk to you," he said.

"Jimmy," I told him, "I'm tired and I want to go to sleep."

"Well," said Peters, "if you don't go, The Rocket will probably come after you."

"Let him come."

Peters left and five minutes later there was another knock on the door. I thought it was Jimmy again so I got up and opened the door.

There stood The Rocket. All he had on was a pair of boxer shorts. God, he looked like an ape. I mean he had more hair over his body than anyone I had ever seen.

There was hair actually sticking up in the air from his shoulders. I knew Rocket was very strong from playing against him, but I never knew he was such a big man. He was very powerful looking, one hell of a physical specimen.

With his very deep French accent, the Rocket said, "Let's go drink some more Courvoisier."

Looking at him, I decided it would not be a good idea to say no, so we went to his room and started talking.

The Rocket said, "My arm was always black-and-blue after I played against you. Why do you always hit me with your stick? My arm's always blue-black from wrist to above the elbow."

I said, "Rocket, when you cut to the net, you always stuck your arm out to hold me off. The only thing I could do was chop you on your arm."

Then The Rocket said, "Did I quit putting my arm out?"

I said, "Yes, Rocket, you did, but it never stopped you from putting the puck in the net!"

Ever since the National Hockey League Players' Association strike of April 1992 there's been a lot of talk about how we older guys had once tried to put together a union. I can speak firsthand about this because I was at the meeting between the owners and players when we originally trying to get something going.

Clarence Campbell was NHL president at the time but I learned the hard way who really was running the league — and it wasn't the president either.

We got into this meeting and Mister Campbell opened the meeting with introductions. Then Conn Smythe, who ran the Toronto Maple Leafs ever since the late 1920's, took over the meeting.

Smythe kept saying, "There will be no damn union in this league as long as I'm a part of it."

We players kept saying that it wasn't a union we had in mind but rather an association.

Still, Smythe remained furious and at least three times

during the meeting, he pounded his fist on the table making all the glasses jump up and down.

When I left the meeting, there was no doubt in my mind — or anyone else's for that matter — who was running the National Hockey League, and it wasn't Clarence Campbell!

A Lady Bynger Turns Badman

Elwin ("Doc") Romnes was a Chicago Black Hawks center of impeccable manners during the late 1930's and, as such, was a winner of the Lady Byng Trophy, awarded for his good sportsmanship and competent play. But in 1938, for a brief moment, Doc turned terrorist on the ice against, of all people, Red Horner, a Toronto Maple Leafs defenseman who was regarded as the meanest man in the National Hockey League.

Romnes, who later was inducted into the United States Hockey Hall of Fame, insisted that he never would have acted so completely out of character had he not been so unabashedly brutalized by Horner during the 1938 Stanley Cup finals between the Black Hawks and Maple Leafs.

"In the first game," Romnes explained, "Horner broke my nose in five places. That game was played in Toronto. I told him that I'd get him in Chicago. Some people thought my coach, Bill Stewart, had something to do with my plan of retaliation but that wasn't true. It was all my idea.

"When the second game was ready to start, I was out for the face-off. I skated up to Horner and swung my stick at his head. Remember, I wasn't that kind of player but in this particular instance I was berserk."

Once the dust had cleared and the penalties meted out, the Black Hawks and Maple Leafs settled down to hockey, and, eventually, Chicago went on to win the Cup. Romnes' hatred for Horner did not abate with the head-knocking at center ice. Doc never thought he would ever wind up playing on the same team as Horner but, lo and behold, Romnes soon learned that he had been traded, of all places, to Toronto where he and his nemesis would share the same locker room.

"We were on our first road trip of the season after we had won the Stanley Cup," said Romnes. "On our way home from Boston our manager, Bill Tobin, sent me word I had been traded to Toronto. That meant Horner and I would be teammates. When the train reached Buffalo, I got off and headed for Chicago. I informed Tobin I was through.

"Back in Chicago, Tobin sent a taxi and asked me down to the office. There was a bonus clause in my contract that stipulated that I be paid $1,500 if I scored a certain number of goals. Tobin told me the bonus would be waiting for me in Toronto if I would report. Well, I couldn't afford to lose $1,500 so I went."

During his journey to Toronto Romnes puzzled over the move. He questioned whether or not he could co-exist on the same team as Horner, particularly in view of their heated clashes. But when Romnes arrived in the Canadian city he was in for a pleasant surprise.

"When I got off the train, the first person I saw was Red Horner. I didn't know what to think. Red removed all my misgivings in a moment. He said: 'C'mon, Doc, from now on you and I are on the same side.' He turned out to be a terrific guy."

Taskmaster with a Capital T
Phil Watson, alias "Phiery Phillipe," was coach of the New York Rangers during the 1958-59 season at a time when the Manhattan sextet was regarded as one of the NHL's best. During mid-February of that year the Rangers not only seemed destined for a playoff berth but were given a fair chance to seriously challenge the Montreal Canadiens for possession of the Stanley Cup.

On a Sunday night at Madison Square Garden the Rangers were leading the Canadiens 1-0, with only ten minutes left to play. Suddenly, the visitors erupted for five goals and defeated New York, 5-1. Livid, Watson entered the loser's dressing room and screamed, "Nobody take off your uniform! We're going back on that ice and do a little skating."

Watson then escorted the players back on to the very ice they had just departed and drove them through every conceivable skating drill. "Up and down," recalled goalie Gump Worsley who was the only Ranger excused from the torture, "side to side. It was terrible punishment, especially after such a tough game. Some reporters who were still in the press box writing their stories couldn't believe it. No coach had ever done such a thing before, and I don't think it's ever been done since."

The extra-curricular activity not only tired the Rangers for the moment but Watson's punishment had a long lasting effect on the team. "It was the homestretch," remembered Camille Henry, the thin left wing who was one of the Rangers' leading scorers, "and we were getting tired. That after-the-game workout that Watson gave us was the straw that broke our backs."

At one point seemingly secure in second place, the Rangers plummeted after that notorious game with the Canadiens. "We dropped to fourth place and the guys were shaky," added Worsley. Yet the Rangers appeared capable of at least securing fourth place, the final playoff berth in the then six-team league. With two weeks left in the schedule they led fifth place Toronto by a comfortable nine points. With five games left in the season the Rangers held a seven point lead over the Maple Leafs. "Then," Worsley concluded, "we went into one of the worst tailspins in history."

Inspired by their coach, Punch Imlach, the Maple Leafs won all of their remaining games while the Rangers annexed but one in their last five. On the final night of the season the Canadiens defeated the Rangers at Madison

Square Garden while Toronto beat the Red Wings at Detroit. Thanks to Watson, the Rangers finished out of the playoffs by one point. "I don't think there was a Ranger who didn't get drunk that night," said Worsley.

As for Watson, he survived through the start of the following season but the specter of the homestretch collapse — and that devastating post-game workout — remained with him. He was fired before the next season was over.

Extra! Extra! Player Sticks Up for Referee!

Jean Baptiste Pusie, an amusing fellow from Chambly, Quebec, once was one of hockey's all-time funnymen during the 1930's. At various times Pusie played for the Montreal Canadiens and New York Rangers as well as numerous minor league teams. Once, while skating for Vancouver in the Pacific Coast League, Pusie watched in horror as Bobby Rowe of the Portland hockey club slugged a referee.

A gallant Gaul, Pusie regarded the act as worthy of a rebuttal. So, on behalf of the official, Pusie walloped Rowe. For some strange reason Pusie's manager, Watterson Patrick, took a dim view of Pusie as the referee-protector. Watterson ordered Pusie to leave the ice, thoroughly infuriating Jean-Baptiste. As he skated to the bench, Pusie broke his stick in twain and tossed the pieces at Patrick's head.

Before word filtered down that league president Cyclone Taylor had suspended Pusie for his indiscretions, Jean Baptiste had boarded an eastbound train. He tarried in Winnipeg long enough to read a telegram from his father in Chambly. There are those who believe that Pere Pusie's letter belongs in the Hockey Hall of Fame. It read: "Jean. Most of the time you are crazy, but this time you are right. Come home at once!"

And he did.

Chapter Three

FUN AND GAMES
IN THE W.H.A.

During the summer of 1971, in the midst of the National Hockey League's glorious expansion period, a communique was transmitted by the national wire services about some chaps in California who hoped to create a new major hockey league. What's more, Gary Davidson and Dennis Murphy, the entrepreneurs in question, were prepared to offer Phil Esposito, the Boston Bruins' scoring machine, $250,000 a year to sign with them.

The story was greeted with loud guffaws around NHL offices. Never since its birth in 1917, had the NHL ever been challenged by a brand-new competitor. Oh, sure, there had been professional teams in Western Canada but they had been around as long, or longer, than the NHL and rightfully challenged for the Stanley Cup. But, a new league. Never!

As it happened, the laughs heard 'round the NHL that summer of 1971 had a boomerang effect. In the end, the laugh was on the NHL for, that winter, the World Hockey Association was officially created at a meeting in New York's Americana Hotel, thereby launching one of the zaniest eras in hockey history. For some it brought nothing but heartache. For others it brought riches. And, for the uninvolved it produced a million laughs until its death in 1979.

The heartache afflicted NHL officials who watched, with awe and anxiety, the component parts of the WHA welded together and then prepare for take-off. "It," announced NHL President Clarence Campbell, "will never get off the ground!"

Sage and revered, the venerable Campbell was rarely wrong. This time he was 180 degrees off target. True, the WHA frequently barked more than it bit, but, one by one, NHL stars expressed an interest in the wads of $1,000 bills waved in their faces by such previously unheard of moguls as Ben (Winnipeg) Hatskin, Howard (Boston) Baldwin and Marvin (New York) Milkes.

One evening Marty Blackman, who was involved with the original New York WHA team, was in pursuit of a manager. He asked a hockey writer-friend for advice. "You need a big name," the reporter advised. "Go for the best. Phone Rocket Richard. See if he's interested."

Blackman got on the blower to Montreal. "Hello, Maurice Richard, would you be interested in managing the New York team in the World Hockey Association?" "What the hell," asked the Rocket, "is the World Hockey Association?"

After listening to a brief explanation, Richard said in so many French-Canadian words, thanks-but-no-thanks, and added that he wanted to see it to believe it. (A few years after the WHA was born, The Rocket was hired to coach the Quebec Nordiques. He quit after a week, it was too hard on his nerves.)

Once Bobby Hull emigrated from Chicago to Winnipeg and signed a multi-million dollar deal with Hatskin's Jets, press conferences sprouted all over the continent with announcements of signings. Some NHL clubs accepted the raids with a frown and others fought back. One afternoon the New York Raiders held a media event to boast that Dave (Hammer) Schultz and Bill (Cowboy) Flett were about to sign with them. Both were property of the NHL's Philadelphia Flyers. Unnoticed, sitting in the back of the room was Gil Stein, the Flyers' attorney. A few weeks later Flett and Schultz were back in Flyers' fold.

The Boston Bruins' weren't as lucky. They lost goalie Gerry Cheevers to Cleveland and defenseman Ted Green to the New England (Boston) Whalers; not to mention Derek Sanderson to the Philadelphia Blazers. The debut of Sanderson and the Blazers at Philadelphia's Civic Center symbolized the future of that team. "We couldn't play our first game," Sanderson remembered, "because they didn't know how to make ice. It cracked wherever we skated so the game had to be called off." A hockey game called because of no-ice. What next?

In point of fact "What next?" became a veritable byword around WHA cities. The league's Los Angeles entry, the Sharks, actually played a game at 11 a.m., which is likely the one and only major hockey match that ever began before noon. It was done because of a television commitment geared to prime Sunday afternoon time in the East.

Then, there was the WHA's Ottawa entry, which turned out to be the rarest of big time franchises; it sold standing room even though the rink wasn't sold out.

Club President Doug Michel explained: "Ottawa was a heavy 'walk-in' town, with people often waiting until the last minute to buy tickets, so we'd get a frantic rush before game time. That's why we sold standing room even though all the seats weren't gone!"

Michel was responsible for introducing one of the zaniest characters ever to put on goalie pads — one Gilles Gratton. In time, Gratton, would play for the Ottawa Nationals, Toronto Toros, Team WHA and, eventually, the NHL's St. Louis Blues and New York Rangers. In each case he would compel his bosses to wonder whatever was the demon spirit that possessed them to sign Gilles in the first place.

At first, Michel believed that he had come up with a netminding prodigy. "We signed him straight out of Junior hockey on a two-year contract for $25,000-$30,000 with a $20,000 bonus," said Michel. "Gilles originally was going to be our 'second' goalie behind the old pro, Les Binkley. But Bink got hurt early in the season and was to play in only 30 games. The bulk of the goaltending was to fall upon the narrow and callow shoulders of the 20-year-old Gratton."

Gilles appeared perfectly normal at first and Michel believed that he had found the second coming of Georges Vezina. But Gilles did not maintain complete decorum for very long is his career.

Grattoony's life was guided, and governed, not by logic but rather by astrological charts. In fact, the Gratton ice saga never would have soared, nor sagged, were it not for a pivotal meeting Gilles had with his personal astrologer in 1970. At the time, Grattoony was playing for the Oshawa (Ontario) Generals of the Ontario Hockey Association Junior "A" division, the foremost Canadian breeding ground for professional players. But Grattoony wasn't sure he should be a hockey player. The one person he went to for guidance was not his coach, or his manager, or his brother Norm, but his astrologer.

The "incredibly different" Grattoony did not really emerge until the Nationals moved to Toronto and became the Toros in 1973. That was when he skated out for practice one day attired solely in his face-mask. Next day's headlines proclaimed: "GRATTON, HOCKEY'S FIRST STREAKER."

"Big deal," said Gilles, recalling the episode. "Streaking was the fad at the time, so I did my thing and it got into the papers. At first the league fined me ten thousand dollars because they thought I streaked in a game. When they found out it was just a practice, the fine was dropped. I wouldn't have done it in a regular game because I knew I'd get thrown right out of the league."

Some WHA officials insisted the Grattoony was worth his salary in publicity alone. In September 1974, when Team Canada was in Stockholm enroute to their Moscow series with the Soviet National Team, Grattoony's photo made every Canadien sports page. While his teammates sat around, Gilles visited the local public sauna. By some strange coincidence, a photographer happened to be there as Grattoony disrobed and a female masseuse arrived. The next day's headlines said: "TOROS' GOALIE POSES NUDE WITH MASSEUSE." And there was a picture of the bare Gratton, his hands covering his groin while Mademoiselle Svenska looked on approvingly.

Gilles allowed a small smile as he recalled this incident. "I was taking my shower and a broad happened to be standing there," he said. "Big deal! It didn't matter to me. I put my hand in front. All they did was take a picture of me with nothing on."

Unlike all WHA players, Gratton was relatively lucky in that he usually received his paychecks on time. Others, such as Andre Lacroix, could not always make that statement. "When I joined the New York Golden Blades," Lacroix revealed, "the league owed me $20,000. For some reason the check was sent to the team instead of me, and before I could get it from them, the owners of the Golden Blades spent the money on a team song. As for the song, I never had a chance to hear it; we were gone out of New York before it came out."

According to hockey writer Reyn Davis of the Winnipeg Free Press, Lacroix was the WHA record holder for "teams (6), homes (8), games (551), assists (547) and total points (798)."

Davis, who followed the WHA better than any other writer from Day One of its existence to its demise, wrote a touching eulogy to the league in an article for Sports Illustrated. "Of the 33 buildings used by the WHA," wrote Davis, "perhaps the worst facility was the Cherry Hill Arena, where the New Jersey Knights played the 29 home games of their brief existence. There were no showers in the visiting team's dressing room, so the opposition had to dress at the Holiday Inn two miles up the road... Most arenas have a long players' bench for each team, but in Cherry Hill the players' section consisted of three rows of five seats. The teams looked like choirs. There was little room for a coach in Cherry Hill, so one night Winnipeg coach Nick Mickoski sat in the first row of the stands. But every time he stood up to make a line change or give instructions to a player, the fans would complain so loudly that he would have to shout his orders sitting down!"

Various WHA coaches employed an assortment of good luck charms to inspire people to come to their buildings as well as collect victories. Easily the most unusual token of good fortune ever used by a team was a half-eaten cob of corn which was spotted outside the Ottawa Nationals' dressing room one night. The club trainer, Peter Unwin, discovered the cob, picked it up, walked into the Nationals' dressing room and tossed it at the first player he saw -

Gavin Kirk. "Hey," said Unwin, "here's a good luck charm I got from an old Indian."

Kirk smiled. "If that's a good luck charm then I guess I better hang onto it. Instead of tossing the cob in the trash can, Kirk placed it in the palm of his glove, which was on the dressing room table behind him. Sure enough, the Nats won 2-1, that night on a screwy goal by Bobby Leduc which deflected off the stick of Bob Wall of the Oilers.

Nats coach Billy Harris was not about to dismiss the cob. "Maybe the lucky lady's going to start smiling in our direction. She's sure as hell been looking the other way."

Following the victory, Kirk returned to the dressing room, spotted the corn cob and placed it carefully in his bag. Who knows, maybe it would work its magic again!

Sure enough, the Nats beat Cleveland, 2-1, and then the New York Raiders, 2-1. Following that, they whipped Chicago, 6-4, for their fourth straight victory, their longest streak of the year. "That dumb corn cob," said Nats owner Doug Michel, "became the focal point of a pre-game ceremony. Before going on the ice Kirk would solemnly remove it from his glove on the dressing room table, have six players rub it for luck, and then pry out one single kernel and throw it to Ken Stephenson. Then everybody'd hoot and holler and charge out onto the ice."

The Nats did so poorly at the gate that there were rumblings the franchise would be moved from Ottawa. Then, Bobby Hull and the Winnipeg Jets came to town and 9,424 people showed up (a near sellout) and prompted needling form the local critics. "The Nationals feel a little uncomfortable," said Ottawa hotelier Sam Koffman, "this is the biggest crowd they've seen all year!"

Hull not only was the Winnipeg franchise, he also kept the league together in its first year, drawing large crowds wherever he skated. This, however, was impossible in the Cherry Hill (New Jersey) Arena, home of the Jersey Knights because how can a rink seating less than 5,000 draw a large crowd? The Cherry Hill Arena was a bandbox among

bandboxes and, according to Hull, featured the most un-
even ice in captivity. "It's the only arena I've ever been to,"
said Hull, "where the visiting team had to skate uphill for
two periods of every game. There was also a huge dip in
the ice."

Reyn Davis reported that a Knights' player, Ted Scharf,
once was awaiting a pass when the puck hit the dip, "shot
straight up and struck him between the eyes."

Disaster seemed to be the WHA's middle name. At the
start of its second season the league held a bizarre exhibition match at Madison Square Garden, featuring the Golden
Blades, Winnipeg Jets and Houston Aeros. It was Gordie
Howe's first WHA appearance and he scored a goal on his
first shift. A gala press party preceded the game but the
fete was marred by the absence of one vital item — food.

The WHA had its share of surprises and flops. A desperate and pathetic attempt was made to produce an ef-
fective black hockey star. Thus, the opportunity came for
Alton White who played in New York but suffered from
mediocrity and never could become a draw at the gate. He
was traded by the Raiders to the Los Angeles Sharks and,
by 1974, was back in the minors.

By contrast, the biggest surprise was Ron Ward, a jour-
neymen NHL defenseman/foward who had played briefly
for the Toronto Maple Leafs and the Vancouver Canucks
before the WHA was organized. Ward was signed by the
Raiders and, by season's end, had racked up 51 goals,
playing on a line with Wayne Rivers and Barton Bradley.
Ward, overnight, had become the toast of hockey. He was
written up in the likes of Sports Illustrated and treated like
a celebrity on Broadway. But before the following season
had ended Ron had been traded three times and, after an
unpleasant tenure with the Cleveland Crusaders, called it
a career.

The WHA finally died with its skates on after Winnipeg defeated Edmonton on May 20, 1979 to win the Avco
World Cup, a trophy donated by a finance company.

At the start, every WHA club had hoped to make it to the NHL but only four —Edmonton, Winnipeg, Quebec City, Hartford— did. Did you recall who didn't?

The Vancouver Blazers, Calgary Cowboys, Toronto Toros, Birmingham Bulls, Ottawa Nationals, Ottawa Civics, New York Raiders, New York Golden Blades, Jersey Knights, Philadelphia Blazers, Baltimore Blades, Cleveland Crusaders, Michigan Stags, Chicago Cougars, Indianapolis Racers, Cincinnati Stingers, Miami Screaming Eagles, Houston Aeros, Minnesota Fighting Saints, Denver Spurs, Phoenix Roadrunners, San Diego Mariners and Los Angeles Sharks.

Chapter Four

ZANY TEAMS

Toronto's Gashouse Gang

Only a thoroughly madcap collection of athletes deserve the affectionate label, "Gashouse Gang." In baseball the tag was fixed on the St. Louis Cardinals and such aces as Pepper Martin, Ducky Medwick, Leo Durocher, and the Dean brothers, Dizzy and Paul. Hockey's answer to the caper-filled Cardinals was the Toronto Maple Leafs, who won the Stanley Cup in 1932 and then proceeded to laugh their way through the Depression years, never winning The Cup again but making a big happy mark that remains today.

The stars of hockey's Gashouse Gang were Charlie Conacher, (Gentleman) Joe Primeau, Harvey (Busher) Jackson, Clarence (Hap) Day, Frank (King) Clancy and Harold (Baldy) Cotton. The chief pranksters among them were Conacher, Clancy and Day who were dubbed "The Three Musketeers of Mirthful Mayhem."

Conacher dominated the Leafs' offense and, to this day, is regarded as one of the fastest skaters from the blue line to the goal. His shot was a blur and his passion for excitement was evident both on and off the ice; but especially when he sat behind the wheel of his cream colored roadster. His boss, Leafs manager Conn Smythe, would marvel at the manner in which Conacher propelled his car along Ontario roads. "Charlie," said Smythe, "used to think driving 80 miles an hour was a canter."

When the Leafs were training in St. Catherines, Ontario, Smythe remembered driving out to see the club and encountering Conacher speeding in the other direction. The Toronto star would beep his boss and, as Conn put it, before Smythe reached his destination Conacher would pass him on his way back!

"Charlie," said author Ed Fitkin who, at one time, was the Leaf's publicist, "had a great zest for life and a great aptitude for deviltry. He and Clancy and Day stopped at nothing when it came to perpetrating gags on their mates. Invariably, Cotton was Conacher's pet fall guy because Cotton was his roommate. Everybody knew of Cotton's fear of height. He suffered so acutely from Acrophobia that he wouldn't go near a window even if it were only one story up. And, naturally, it was the inspiration for a great many of the gags."

Once, following a heated argument that began on the Toronto-to-New York train, Conacher became angry over Cotton's complaints over Charlie's failure to deliver a pass. By the time they reached their New York City hotel, Conacher was at wit's end. After unpacking in their room, Cotton and Conacher reached a new high in decibel count whereupon Charlie grabbed Cotton in a bear hug and carried him to the window. "Admit I'm right," Conacher asserted, "or I'll drop you out of the window."

"You can't scare me," Cotton fired back.

"Okay," Conacher replied , "you asked for it. Here goes..."

Conacher appeared unconcerned that the room in Manhattan's Hotel Lincoln (on Eighth avenue near Times Square) was 20 floors above the sidewalk.

"Conacher," Cotton remembered, "yanked me to the window, got a good grip on my legs, and hung me, head down, out in the wild blue yonder. There I was dangling 20 floors above the pavement, and I was supposed to be in good physical and mental condition to play hockey that evening. I began to holler and they probably heard me over in Brooklyn."

Determined to win an apology from Cotton, Conacher allowed his teammate to drop an inch or two more. "With that," said Cotton, "I gave in and promised to be a good Maple Leaf."

Satisfied with Cotton's statement of surrender, Conacher lifted his pal back through the window, but not before giving Baldy and a few other Leafs the shock of their lives. As it happened, Joe Primeau and Busher Jackson were in the room below and leaped to their feet at the sight of their upside down pal. "You can imagine what a shock we got seein' Baldy hanging out the window," said Primeau. "He looked like a ghost and was yelling like a madman."

Those close to Cotton report that Baldy's acrophobia took a turn for the worse after that experience. "You couldn't get him near a window," said Fitkin, "not even for love, money, or his pants."

On another occasion Cotton was in bed when Clancy and Conacher entered his room. Before Baldy could make a move, the impish pair seized his trousers and hung them out of the hotel room window. Cotton screamed in despair but made no move to grab his trousers even though they contained his wallet. Meanwhile, Conacher and King Clancy conducted an orderly retreat leaving Cotton and his pants alone together. Too frightened to approach the window, Baldy simply waited in bed.

Within a half hour another of Cotton's teammates knocked on the door and Baldy invited him in, while remaining in bed. "Would you mind handing me my pants?" Cotton asked, pretending that he had just awoken from a deep sleep.

"Sure Baldy, where'd you put 'em?" the other asked.

"Oh, I forgot, I hung 'em out the window. Wanted to air 'em."

The teammate retrieved the pants and, once again, Cotton was a free man. Curiously, Baldy never seemed sufficiently intimidated by the larger Conacher to call a moratorium on provoking Charlie. With what almost seemed to be a masochistic bent, Cotton insisted upon engaging Conacher in battle. Once, after a lengthy argument, the perturbed Conacher was tempted to storm out of the hotel room but before doing so he turned a bed upside down on Cotton, pinning him to the floor. To be sure that Baldy could not escape, Charlie strategically placed a number of pillows around his victim and fortified these with heavy chairs. Conacher then moved the two desks over to the barricade and bade Cotton good-bye. As he departed, Charlie removed the phone from the hook.

Before Conacher could get to the elevator, Cotton began bellowing for help and, eventually, a house detective, hearing the screams, broke into the room and rescued the manacled Maple Leaf.

Although Clancy often was a perpetrator of pranks he eventually wound up being victimized. Once, King was in his hotel room with some of his buddies, and in a semi-nude condition. It was then that Clancy began to boast about his excellent body.

Neither Hap Day nor the unimpressionable Conacher were awed by Clancy's physique but they were determined to exploit his braggadocio. Day and Conacher wrestled Clancy over to the balcony, opened the door, and shoved King out onto the open porch where he was in full view of the pedestrians below. "You've got such a wonderful physique," snapped Day, "then you should be able to stay out there all night and not even feel the cold."

From time to time even the Bunyanesque Conacher would find himself on the wrong end of a prank. One night, Charlie dressed himself up to the nines in preparation for a night on the town. Finally, ready to go, Conacher pulled his suit into place and strutted out the door whereupon he was covered with four gallons of water. Hap Day had waited for two hours outside the door to perpetrate the ploy.

Once, during a training camp, the entire roster — with the notable exception of Primeau — attended a party. Upon their return to the Leafs' base, the players entered their respective rooms and discovered that each and every bed sheet had been knotted tighter than a stale pretzel. The obvious culprit was Primeau since he had not attended the fete. Enraged, the Toronto players tiptoed to Joe's room, unhooked a fire hose and placed the nozzle through a transom. In a trice, Primeau was well-watered. "I thought the place was on fire," said Joe, "but when I saw those monkeys out in the hall, I really blew my top."

Undaunted, Primeau soon wiped himself dry and then explained to his chums that he did not tie the sheets. Soon, they were convinced and set about the business of finding the real culprit. Since Clancy was the first to point an accusing finger at Primeau, King was assumed to be the culprit.

In no time at all Clancy was trapped and hurled into a running shower — with his clothes on! King got drenched protesting his quasi-innocence to the end. Only days later did he reveal who had masterminded the scheme. "Hap Day was the guy who dreamed up that one. We slipped away from the party without letting anyone see us go, went back to the hotel, knotted every sheet we could lay our hands on, and then headed back to the party without anybody realizing we were gone."

Since nearly all long-distance trips in those days were made by train — usually overnight trains requiring sleeping cars — the players had ample time to plot their pranks. One of the best — or worst, depending on one's viewpoint — was the incident on a train trip from Montreal to Toronto. Most of the players, with the exception of Conacher and Primeau, were engaged in card games — a fact that did not elude the mischievous Conacher. He took Primeau by the arm and walked him into the empty players' Pullman. "Joe," he said, pointing to the bags which had been heaved on to the berths, "we have them at our mercy."

While Primeau looked on, Conacher began transferring clothes from one valise to another. "You never saw such a mess," said Primeau. "I was enjoying the gag myself until I suddenly realized that I might be singled out as the guilty party." Joe made his exit just as Conacher pulled the switch turning off all the lights on the Pullman.

"I knew what Conacher would do when the gang found their clothes and bags all mixed up," said Primeau. "He'd just pass it off by saying 'I don't see that guy Primeau around here anywhere and everybody would be gunning for me. I sat in the club car until we passed Smith Falls (more then half-way home) and I didn't go back to our car until I figured everybody would be too sound asleep to care."

As carefree as the Gashouse Leafs were off the ice, they were as determined on the ice. They fought hard and well except for the diminutive Clancy who held the unofficial NHL record of never having won a single fight. "King always claimed that he won one fight," said Primeau. "He said he poked Eddie Shore on the chops one night and then skated away before Eddie could get back at him. But no one believed him."

Clancy's fistic record was so atrocious that his teammates finally took it upon themselves to arrange a victory for him. They decided to wait for an opportunity where King was at least fighting a draw and then help Clancy take the bout. The opportunity arose one night when King and an opponent got into a wrestling match. "Here's our chance," Conacher yelled over to Jackson. The two Leafs grabbed Clancy and moved him into a position where he couldn't help but fall on top of his foe; then they skated away, assuming that with King on top he would take the bout. But before they had skated 20 feet away, Jackson turned and tapped Conacher: "Don't look now, Charlie, but King's on the bottom again!"

The Macon Whoopees
In the early 1970's, a hockey boom swept North America, from coast to coast, from the North to the South. Such once frigid outposts as Phoenix, Arizona, and Atlanta, Georgia were represented in organized hockey so it no longer was surprising when a team was established south of the Mason-Dixon line. But by far one of the strangest franchises in any sport was created in the city of Macon, Georgia.

It was there that the Macon Whoopees became a presence in the Southern Hockey League, and for a brief moment in the history of the stick and puck, created a cockeyed saga of why fools rush in and buy sports clubs where (financial) angels fear to tread. Many people, including a man named Robert Fierro, believed the Macon Whoopees should never have been created. But that is what this saga is all about; the team *that shouldn't have been*. The adventure began in a New York City tavern, circa February 1974.

Fierro, a hockey fan who was once a public relations consultant, had worked with a chap named Gerald C. Pinkerton, a financial consultant, in organizing the Southern League. The league was launched with teams from Charlotte, Greensboro, Roanoke, St. Petersburg, and Winston-Salem.

Somehow, a sixth city was deemed necessary to round out the circuit and Macon, a molasses-slow town 60 miles from Atlanta, was chosen.

Now that the last-needed franchise was found, the league had to find an owner for Macon's new entry. Southern League governors urged Pinkerton to take the team, but he declined. However, a conversation with Fierro turned things around. The phone dialogue went like this:

"They want me to buy a hockey team," said Pinkerton.

"So?," countered Fierro.

"What am I going to do with a hockey team?"

"Look, you've always wanted to be in sports. You're a hockey nut. The fact that you aren't rich shouldn't hinder you. Form a syndicate. Buy the damn team."

"In Macon?"

"Why not? You could always call them the Macon Whoopees!"

Fierro swears that that's exactly how the club name came into being. Then, it turned out that Pinkerton's favorite song was Doris Day's recording of Gus Kahn's classic tune, "Makin' Whoopee!"

Pinkerton still wasn't sure he should get into hockey.

He turned to his neighbor at the bar for advice. The neighbor happened to be Tim Ryan, the NBC's play-by-play broadcaster for the NHL Game of the Week.

"If you had a hockey team," asked Pinkerton, "in Macon, Georgia, what would you name them?"

"I like the Macon Eggs," Ryan shot back.

"Would you believe the Macon Whoopees?," snapped Pinkeron.

Ryan's eyes lit up. "If you do THAT I'll give your scores on the air every week and make you the Slippery Rock of hockey."

Pinkerton was sold on the idea. So, he bought the team, named them the Macon Whoopees and signed one of pro hockey's all-time flakes, Cleland "Keke" Mortson, as G.M./Coach. "The on-ice battle cry of the team," Fiero recalled, "Became Keke, Keke, Keke-Whooooopeee."

Everybody, from local newscasters to the city fathers, loved the Whoopees. So did the Wall Street Journal and Sports Illustrated, each of which mentioned the team with affection, as did the national wire services. The whole hockey world, it seemed, was ga-ga over the Whoopees. The only trouble was that nobody went to see them at the 7,500 seat coliseum.

A big mistake, Fierro insisted, was scheduling home games on Wednesday and Sunday nights. "Those," he explained, "were church nights. The people didn't necessarily go to church or stay home. But their money stayed home."

The Whoopees remained in second place for most of the first half of the season, although the players frequently did not get paid (attendance averaged only 1,100) and the promotion manager suffered a nervous breakdown brought on by malnutrition.

The end was in sight, and finally, in February 1974 the Macon Whoopees played their final game.

"The ice melted," said Fierro, "and so did a lot of wallets, mine included!"

Although many have made light of the adventure, the fact remains that the Whoopees brief rise and sudden fall holds significant symbolism for hockey promotion. It took place during an era of too rapid hockey expansion for which the NHL and the now defunct WHA paid dearly.

In a serious moment, Fierro summed up the lesson that was learned and hopefully remembered in the future by other prospective promoters. To wit:

"The games that little boys invent have turned into games that other little boys in pinstripe suits play. A little boy must understand that just because he owns the puck, that doesn't mean the other little boys are going to play with him. The result could be a Fire in Chicago, a Storm in Portland or Sharks washed up on the beach in Jacksonville.

"There was lots of whoopee in Macon, but there was no makin' money. There are other reasons, and there will be other seasons. But if you're harboring the thought of plunging into professional sports ownership, you'd better keep 'em. I think it's cheaper to make your own kind of whoopee!"

A Probibition Bootlegger and his NHL Team

One of the flakiest teams ever to step on NHL ice arrived in New York City by way of Hamilton, Ontario. It was owned by a Manhattan bootlegger named William (Big Bill) Dwyer and cut one of the wildest swaths big-time hockey has known.

The New York Americans wore flamboyant, star-spangled jerseys matching in color their behavior both on and off the ice. They never won the Stanley Cup and never finished first, yet from their birth in 1925 to their unfortunate death in 1942 they captured the imagination of all who adored the underdog.

Curiously, it was a Canadian-born newspaperman covering sports in New York City who inspired bootlegger Dwyer to launch the Americans, William McBeth, a sportswriter from Windsor, Ontario, believed that if hockey could be properly staged in Manhattan it would be an instant hit. McBeth had his listeners and his backers but he lacked one item: a major league arena. That, however, was supplied when Tex Richard and his "Six Hundred Millionaires" built the "new" Madison Square Garden on Eighth Avenue and 49th Street in the early twenties.

McBeth realized that even though the new Garden had flaws (built primarily for prize-fighting it lacked adequate sight-lines for hockey) there were 15,000 seats and enough ones to satisfy even the most discriminating hockey fan. But the Garden backers were ignorant and, consequently, dubious about hockey's potential so McBeth had to go elsewhere for money.

His choice was Dwyer, a character among characters in that era of wonderful nonsense. A native New Yorker, the potbellied Dwyer grew up in the area around the new Garden, living the life of a quasi-Dead-End Kid. He did a short stretch at Sing Sing Penitentiary and bounced around the West Side of Manhattan until Prohibition arrived; Dwyer's big moment came precisely then.

While others warily wondered whether to plunge into the gold mine of rum-running and other "industries" created by the new law, Big Bill made his move fast — and the money rolled in even faster. By the mid-twenties Dwyer's empire comprised a couple of night clubs, race tracks, a fleet of ships and trucks, as well as warehouses and a full-fledged gang appropriately stocked with the Jimmy Cagneys and Edward G. Robinsons of the day.

As far as McBeth was concerned, Dwyer was the perfect choice to back his team because Big Bill liked sports and wanted very much to improve his image by owning a hockey club. A little prestige never hurt any bootlegger and owning the Americans promised a lot of it, possibly even the Stanley Cup as well.

The next step was finding a team. This, too was accomplished in a typically bizarre manner. During the

1924-25 NHL season the Hamilton Tigers went out on strike, marking one of the few times in sports history that a team ever marched on a picket line.

Led by Red Green, Hamilton players objected that the season was lengthened from 24 to 30 games yet they had received no increase in salary. They demanded a $200 boost per man and got instead nothing but a stiff rebuke and $200 individual fines from President Frank Calder. The Hamilton players remained firm in their strike and early in April 1925 league governors got wind of both their strike and Dwyer's desire to own a hockey team. They reasoned that the Hamilton problem could be simply resolved by selling the franchise to the Manhattan bootlegger and on April 17, 1925, it was agreed at an NHL meeting that the Hamilton club would be transplanted to New York at the start of the 1925-26 season.

The deal was officially confirmed on September 22, 1925, at a league conference in New York. Dwyer obtained both the franchise and the suspended players — quite appropriately he bought them even though their suspension had never been lifted— for $75,000. Thomas Patrick "Tommy" Gorman, one of Canada's more ebullient personalities, was chosen as manager and the new team promptly was named the Americans — and just as quickly nicknamed the Amerks by space-conscious headline writers.

If Big Bill Dwyer was pleased, Bill McBeth was in his glory. The dream of bringing major league hockey to New York City was realized on December 15, 1925, when the Montreal Canadiens faced the Americans in the opening NHL game at Madision Square Garden.

Although the new Garden had already been open for business, the hockey premiere was greeted with the same respect and heraldry as the opening of the Metropolitan Opera House. Dignitaries from both countries jammed the arena, most wearing white tie and tails. Marching bands paraded impeccably across the ice and then the Canadiens defeated the Americans 3-1, a fact immediately forgotten in the waves of champagne poured by Big Bill Dwyer during his post-game party.

When the Amerks finally drifted off cloud nine and back to the reality of a 36-game schedule they played competitive if not championship hockey. Billy Burch scored 19 goals and finished seventh in the league; such redoubtables as the Green brothers — Shorty and Ed — defensemen Leo Reise, Sr., and Alec McKinnon, and the peripatetic "Bullet" Joe Simpson gave New Yorkers plenty to cheer about.

Rather appropriately, McBeth was named publicity director of the team and while successfully trumpeting their virtues throughout the Metropolitan Area he also helped to produce the Americans' artistic downfall that first year. It happened because McBeth chose to single out Burch and Simpson for the loudest drum-beating. He christened Simpson "The Blue Streak from Saskatoon" and Burch "The Babe Ruth of Hockey." New Yorkers, unschooled in hockey fundamentals, seized upon the nicknames and immediately made these two their favorites, demanding a goal from them each time Billy or Joe would touch the puck.

Conscious of their newly created audience, Burch and Simpson responded by stressing their individual exploits. "Every time one of them passed to another player," wrote Frank Graham, Sr., who covered sports for the New York Sun, "the spectators howled in rage and disappointment. Seeking to please the customers, Billy and Joe did as little passing as possible. This resulted in spectacular but futile one-man raids on the enemies' nets and a rapid disintegration of the team play necessary to insure victories as the other players then all tried to get into the act as individuals."

A mild case of dissension followed, principally because Shorty Green was so ardent a team player that he couldn't accept the "playing-to-the-crowd" style of his colleagues. "There were frequently tears in his eyes following a losing game." noted Graham. "But nobody else seemed to care."

Nobody had time to care; the abundant distractions for the now adored Canadian boys kept them equally busy off-ice. Just a block away from the Garden sat the glittering White Way of Times Square with its wine, women, and song — mostly the first two temptations. Occasionally, Dwyer's bootleg hooch would find its way into the Amerks' dressing room with amusing results. One such incident occurred at the conclusion of the 1925-26 season. New York had finished in fifth place, respectably ahead of Toronto and the Canadiens, and had scheduled a post-season exhibition game at Madison Square Garden just prior to the arrival of the Ringling Bros. Barnum and Bailey Circus.

As was normally the case, circus officials moved their animals into the Garden menagerie several days before the show opened and in this instance the floating zoo was located about a hundred feet from the teams' dressing room toward the rear of the arena.

Following the exhibition match with Portland, the Americans were greeted with a case of bootleg booze which Simpson eagerly poured. After a few hearty rounds, "Bullet Joe" left the dressing room and walked straight into the menagerie where he was greeted by a trumpeting elephant and several boisterous lions. Stunned to the core, Simpson wheeled in his tracks and fled back to the dressing room where he grabbed Percy Ryan, the Americans' trainer.

"Where in hell did that bad hooch come from?" Joe demanded. "Christ! I could swear I saw a herd of wild elephants out there."

Though there were plenty of laughs, the Americans had managed to become a serious business proposition. In their first year they had proven hockey could be a money-maker in Manhattan and had underscored this with enough big crowds to inspire the Madision Square Garden Corporation to get into the act with a team of its own. This was easy to do because the Garden already was collecting a healthy rental from the Amerks — it also shared in their gate receipts — and the emergence of another New York team would create a stimulating rivalry, matching the Giants and Dodgers in baseball.

Dwyer was making too much money on bootlegging at the time to care but the Garden already was beginning to force his hand. When he first decided to bring the team to New York he had been assured that the Garden would never install a club of its own — and now the high rent and other expenses eventually would hasten his downfall. But with the demand for illegal booze at an all-time high and an income too big to even count, Big Bill couldn't care less about what the Garden was doing to him.

The same carefree attitude characterized his player's deportment. Gorman had signed former great Newsy Lalonde as coach for the 1926-27 season but even so awesome a personality as Lalonde couldn't control the laugh-happy Amerks. Their behavior was so notorious that even the official NHL history took note in its 1926-27 edition with the following observation: "Newsy Lalonde has his hands full with his rollicking crew of Americans who were living it up on Broadway. (Lionel) Conacher and Burch were suspended for breaking training after their loss to Detroit on March 15th."

Suspensions hardly proved a deterrent especially when Conacher was involved. Once, he was playing cards in a hotel room with Billy Burch when Red Green tossed an apple core and hit Conacher on the head. Lionel jumped out of his chair and pursued Red down the hall until the elusive Green dashed into an empty room, locking the door behind him.

Conacher, who later was to be voted Canada's Athlete of the Half Century, reared back and charged at the door. In the process his shoulder rammed the door frame plus the wall and buckled the floor supports so badly that the hockey club had to pay $500 in repairs.

When the Americans weren't fighting among themselves they managed pretty well against the opposition, especially the Rangers. What made this rivalry so keen though he had a couple of young prospects in goaltender Chuck ("Bonnie Prince Charlie") Rayner and Pat (Boxcar) Egan.

Dutton had high hopes for Egan who was a hard hitter and a good shooter for a backliner. However, when his play fell below expected standards, Dutton believed that his prodigy was being distracted by Broadway showgirls and cabaret whiskey.

"A bottle of beer once in a while never hurt a hockey player," Dutton cautioned Egan, "but the hard stuff'll kill you. Pat, lay off that booze."

But in his next game, Egan was worse than ever and Dutton invited him to his office for a private conference. The boss demanded to know what the problem was and Egan immediately replied, "I don't understand it. Mr. Dutton, do you know Jack White?"

Of course, Dutton knew Jack White. He ran a bar near the Garden. "What's he got to do with it?" Dutton demanded.

"Well," Egan went on, "I went to see him yesterday and, like you told me, I wouldn't drink that whisky. I only drank beer. Then I ate and I was at the Garden in plenty of time for the game."

"I'm not so sure about beer BEFORE a game," Dutton said. "How many did you have?"

"Oh," blurted Egan, "a dozen or so — but no booze!"

Booze or no booze, the Americans finished last in 1941-42 after which the club was disbanded for the duration of World War II. Dutton eventually became NHL president a year later but his heart was with the Americans; so much so that during the war he began making plans for their return when hostilities ceased in Europe and Asia.

Dutton's dream was to build a brand new arena for the Amerks in Brooklyn where they would be side by side with the Dodgers battling the enemy in Manhattan. The Canadiens, Black Hawks and Red Wings supported Red and it appeared as if the Americans would rise again when the league met to consider Dutton's bid in 1946

Red resigned the presidency and then awaited a decision on his new Brooklyn franchise. As Trent Frayne noted in his book, *The Mad Men of Hockey*, Dutton fully expected approval based on promises he had received in the past. But when Red asked Conn Smythe, the Leafs governor, whether everything had gone well, Smythe shook his head.

"There are complications," said Smythe.

As it happened, Madison Square Garden, owner of the Rangers, no longer wanted any competition in the New York area. The Garden successfully lobbied the other owners to put the nix on Dutton's Brooklyn bid and, then and there, the Americans died.

Typically, Dutton breathed fire before walking out of the conference room. "I looked around the room," he recalled, "but nobody was looking at me. I got the message. 'Gentlemen,' I said to the governors, 'You can stick your franchise up your ass.' I gathered my papers and left!"

The Rollicking Rangers

The New York Rangers were admitted into the National Hockey League in 1926 and, almost from the beginnning, they earned a reputation for zaniness above and beyond the call of duty. In fact, the first madcap episode occurred before the team actually began it's initial season.

Conn Smythe, who later quit the Ranger organization for the Toronto Maple Leafs, was called upon to organize the Manhattan sextet. Since Smythe was a native of Toronto, he ordered that the training camp be held there and designated the Peacock Hotel, on the outskirts of town, as the club's base.

A military-minded man, Smythe ordered a strict curfew for his incoming players and warned them that the hotel door would be locked after midnight. One of the

Ranger hopefuls was a defenseman named Ivan "Ching" Johnson. "He came from a part of the country," said *Globe and Mail* columnist Jim Coleman, "where they didn't even know how to spell the word curfew. Johnson arrived in Toronto with a cargo of luggage that consisted almost entirely of Jersey applejack."

In a matter of minutes, Johnson befriended Frank Boucher, another new Ranger who enjoyed a good gag, and the two of them left the hotel for a long discussion of the coming season and other such matters as their mutual dislike of curfews. By the time early morning approached, both Boucher and Johnson had decided they should consult with Smythe about his unfair and unwarranted curfew. They hailed a cab and returned to the Peacock Hotel, only to discover that, as Smythe had warned, the door was locked tight.

Undaunted, the pair attempted to climb the fire escape and make their way through an open window, but they both lost their footing on the ladder and fell to the ground. Fortunately the applejack went unharmed. They decided there was only one thing to do — return to mid-town Toronto.

The pair carried on through the early morning. At about 6:00 A.M. they found themselves at a major intersection where a trolley was about to begin it's first run of the morning. The Ranger duo climbed aboard and discovered that the motorman was a jolly chap, so out came the applejack. The three of them stood on the trolley guzzling to the tune of "Sweet Adeline."

Finally the motorman realized it was time to begin his trip. But he had his two customers to think of. "Where you guys goin'?" he asked. Boucher suggested that they would head for the King Edward Hotel, where they decided they would stay for the rest of the morning.

The hotel didn't happen to be on the route prescribed by the Toronto Transit Commission, but that didn't seem to bother the motorman. He turned off the overhead lights, threw open the control lever, and away they sped. Three

blocks later a half-dozen potential passengers stood waiting for the streetcar to stop and pick them up, when to their
amazement it roared by like the Twentieth Century Lim-
ited.

Soon the Transit Commision began receiving irate calls
from the passengers who insisted that their trolley car had
rolled past the stop without so much as decelerating. Fifteen minutes after the motorman began his mad ride, he
realized that in order to reach the King Edward he would
have to switch tracks. When the trolley car reached the
next switch, the motorman stopped the streetcar, walked
out with a huge steel crowbar, threw the switch, clambered
back aboard, and started the car again. The trolley swerved
right at the switch and sped onto the downtown tracks.
Five minutes later, the three musketeers arrived directly in
front of the King Edward Hotel.

Delighted with his gesture, the motorman opened the
doors, stepped out like a genuine chauffeur, and escorted
them into the King Edward to finish their applejack.

"To this day," said Boucher in retrospect, "we never
found out if he got back to the right route or whether his
job survived that run."

Boucher and Johnson weren't the only practical jokers on that team. Another was Leo Bourgeault, who joined
the team after manager Conn Smythe had been replaced
by Lester Patrick — the "silver fox" of hockey — in 1926.
Like Smythe, Patrick was a martinet who demanded strict
obedience from his charges. He, too, was particularly rigid
regarding curfews.

One night the Rangers were in Ottawa for a game with
the old Senators. Patrick had warned the players to be back
on the team's pullman by 1:00A.M.

"We won the game something like 10-1," said
Bourgeault, later a successful tavern owner in Quebec
City, "and decided to celebrate with a party in Hull across
the river."

Feeling no pain, the players returned from the party to
the pullman car near dawn. Despite their condition, they

were coherent enough to know that they had to tiptoe into the train or there would be trouble. "Don't wake Lester," was the word passed up and down the line, and the "coup" seemingly went well.

The next morning Bourgalt strolled into the diner, where the implacable Lester was hunched over a dish of bacon and eggs.

"Good morning, Mr. Bourgeault," said Lester, who always addressed players by their last names when they were in trouble. After a few minutes of hemming and hawing by Bourgeault, Lester offhandedly remarked, "Leo, did you know Butch Keeling walks in his sleep?"

Leo said no. Whereupon Lester explained that Keeling had walked into his compartment at about four in the morning, spilled a quantity of liquor, and murmured, barely above a whisper, "Don't wake Lester!"

Another amusing incident involving Patrick occurred when Cecil Dillon, one of the best old-time Ranger scorers, met with him to negotiate a contract. The veterans had told the rookie Cecil that during the meeting it would be wise to give Lester the impression that he was a year or two younger than he actually was so he would be able to stay in the league longer. Dillon agreed with this idea. An hour after his meeting with Patrick, Dillon was approached by the other Rangers. "Did you subtract a year?" they asked.

"I certainly did," Dillon replied with fresh confidence. "I told Lester I was born in 1907 instead of 1908."

Chapter Five

PRANKS

They Never Change
Ever since the early days of professional hockey the prank
has been as much a part of the woof and warp of the game
as a stick and puck. One time-honored tradition that has
lasted to the present is welcoming former teammates to
town by vandalizing their equipment.

A perfect example of such shenanigans was provided
by the Quebec Nordiques and St.Louis Blues in St.Louis on
Thanksgiving Day 1991.

At the time Tony Twist was with Quebec and Kelly
Chase with St.Louis. They had previously been teammates
on the Blues.

Twist checked in with his fellow Nordiques and his
equipment, miraculously, went untouched.

The scenario then switched to Le Colisée in Quebec
where the Blues were visiting Les Nordiques later in the
season.

Chase arrived at the Blues practice and discovered that
the laces on his skates were sliced, there was Vaseline on his
helmet and shaving cream sprayed inside his hockey gloves.

"That Twister got me," moaned Chase, wiping the
Vaseline out of his helmet.

Chase planned a revenge ambush of his own and Twist
was well aware that there might be a strike made against
his equipment. He tried to prevent it by pulling the name-
plate off his locker and switching it with Adam Foote's on
a neighboring locker. But there was a hitch; Foote's number

52 was written all over the equipment."

"That's okay," Twist said, "Kelly's not that smart!"

Mike Gartner's Favorite Practical Joke

When I was with the Washington Capitals we used to leave our cars at the team's practice rink before going on road trips. After the trip was over the guys would return to the rink and get their cars.

We were on a road trip but left goalie Pete Peeters and defenseman John Barrett at home because they had been injured. One day Barrett and Pete Peeters were working out at the practice rink. After they finished their workout, they decided to pull a fast one on Dale Hunter so that when he returned from the trip, he wouldn't be able to drive his car out of the lot.

What they did was somehow to jack his car up on blocks just enough so that when he got into the car Dale wouldn't realize that it was on blocks. Meanwhile, they arranged it so that the back tires were off the ground.

Those guys did a perfect job because when we got home from the road trip, Hunter got in the car and had no idea anything had been tampered with while he was away.

He turned the ignition key on and started the motor. Then he shifted into reverse and put his foot on the accelerator but the darn car wouldn't move. Next he put it in first gear and it still wouldn't go forward. It wouldn't do anything!"

That's when he got out and finally realized that his car was on blocks. The rest of us had to take it back down again.

Ed Mio Tells How "Cowboy" Flett Relaxed Him

When I was with the Edmonton Oilers in 1979 I would get very tense before I went out on the ice to play goal.

Bill ("Cowboy") Flett figured out how to relax me one day. I was getting ready to get dressed and found a live mouse in my skate. Then when I tried to put my gloves on there was a snake stuck in one of the gloves.

Dave Brown's Favorite Toll Bridge Prank

When I was with the Philadelphia Flyers, Greg Smyth was a rookie defenseman and we used to get him good in every which way.

One of the first things we told him was that as a member of the Flyers, he didn't have to pay a toll on the bridges leading to The Spectrum, where we played our home games.

Smyth must have figured that hockey players get a lot of breaks just because they were hockey players and the bridge toll freebie was just another one. So, on his first trip to The Spectrum with a few of us in the back of the car, he pulled it up to the toll booth on the Walt Whitman Bridge and yelled over at the clerk to lift the gate for him because he's a Flyer.

But nobody lifted any gate. Instead, a security guard walked over to Greg's car and asked him what the trouble was all about.

"Jesus Christ," yelled Smyth, "I'm with the Flyers; let me through here."

The security guard was getting madder by the second. "Listen, buddy, you'd better get your money out or you're not getting through."

Smyth yelled right back at him until he realized that we were laughing our heads off in the back and then he got the message.

Marcel Dionne Remembers Bugsy

There was a little guy named Bryan Watson who bounced all over the NHL from the Canadiens to the Capitals to the Red Wings. He could play defense and he could play forward and he always was bugging the opposition, so maybe that's why he was nicknamed Bugsy.

You had to watch him every minute he was on the ice — and every minute off the ice as well because he was full of tricks. Bugsy thought nothing of putting frogs in my skates,

baby powder in my pants and Vaseline on the phone when
he knew I was going to make a call.

One of his best gags took place when we went out to
some nice restaurant for dinner. I'd check my coat and then
take a seat at our table.

At some point during the meal, Watson would excuse
himself, saying he had to go to the john. Of course, he wasn't
really going to the toilet; at least I learned that later.

What he did was gather a lot of silverware somewhere in
the restaurant and put it in my coat pocket. After dinner,
when I went to the checkroom to get my coat, Bugsy would
call the waitress and tell her about the guy — me! — who
was stealing all the knives, forks and spoons. He was setting
me up all the time.

Joe Watson Exposes Bobby Clarke

Clarkie was somebody you wanted to watch out for if you
knew what was good for you. Our goalie, Wayne Stephenson,
wasn't watching out well enough on this road trip.

It was the middle of the winter and, let me tell you, it was
frigid by the time we got to Minnesota. It must have been
ten-below while we about to land at the Minneapolis Airport.

Wayne didn't know it but Clarkie had very craftily got
hold of Stephenson's suit and cut off one pant leg. There's
Wayne walking through the Minnesota airport with one
pant leg on and one pant leg off; it was a sight to behold.

The funny part of it was that Clarkie always managed to
wear the most innocent look of all the fellas on the team, but
most of us knew that he had instigated most of the pranks.

The Stolen Car Routine

Naive rookies invariably are the targets of practical jokers as
Mario Tremblay, now a Canadiens broadcaster, learned when
he was a Montreal freshman.

It was 1974 and the young forward celebrated his first
Habs contract by purchasing a new car. Before every prac-

tice at The Forum, Mario carefully deposited his most prized possession at the Plaza Alexis Nihon parking garage across the street from the arena.

One morning, Tremblay decided to work overtime on his skills and remained on the ice long after the veterans had left the rink. Having completed his drills, Mario then showered, donned civilian clothes and crossed the street to get his car.

When he arrived at the garage there was an empty space where the sedan should have been sitting. The kid's worst nightmare had come true; his new car was gone along with his valuables and his driver's license.

Mario quickly phoned the police, contacted his car dealer and helped launch an investigation for the missing automobile. Meanwhile, Mario fretted and fretted some more.

By this time his older teammates noticed the rookie's depression and became concerned enough to take action. An anonymous letter appeared in Tremblay's locker which detailed the precise location of the "missing" car.

Mario high-tailed it to the destination and, sure enough, totally unharmed and still spanking new was the Tremblay vehicle.

Shortly thereafter, veteran defenseman Guy Lapointe owned up to the prank, one of hundreds he pulled during his long stint with the Canadiens.

The Nick Fotiu Capers
It would require a battery of psychologists to explain precisely what makes a professional hockey player a practical joker. Nick Fotiu is an interesting case in point.

A native of Staten Island, New York, Fotiu learned his hockey on rinks ranging from Manhattan to Long Island and eventually worked his way to the World Hockey Association. From there, Nick made the successful jump to the NHL and became an instant fan favorite with New York Rangers rooters.

His charisma was based on the spectators immediately

immediately sensing that Fotiu was a gregarious, fun-loving type who never failed to toss several pucks up to the distant balcony-ites in the cheapseats.

What the fans didn't know was that Nicky was a compulsive practical joker who would do anything to get a laugh out of his teamates — even at their own expense.

Nicky's standard gag was the dollar-bill string routine. When the Rangers were waiting in the airport for a flight, he would sit in the terminal with a piece of string in his hand. The string would be about 20 feet long and snake along the floor of the waiting room. At the very end of it a ten dollar bill was attached.

To a passing commuter, the bill was readily observable but the thin string was virtually camouflaged by the floor. Invariably, someone would see the ten-spot, lean over to pick it up and — poof! just like that — Fotiu would yank the string and pull it away, much to the consternation of the victim and utter delight of Nicky's teammates.

"Nick had a lot of specialties," said John Ferguson, who managed the Rangers when Fotiu played for New York. "Once we were on a flight and I made the mistake of falling asleep while Nick was still awake. He sneaked up to my seat and covered my face with shaving cream. I must have had a pretty good dream because I didn't feel a thing. Then, he sprinkled some nut on top of the cream and, dammit, don't you think he then had the nerve to take a photo of his general manager, a la mode! When I finally awakened under my mixed covering, I stared him down and said, 'You've come a long way in two weeks, rookie.'"

Occasionally, Nick's teammates would be bothered by flickering lights in their hotel rooms. When they'd phone the manager with complaints, they would be told that nothing was wrong with the hotel's electrical system. How would the manager know that crafty Nick, after a diligent search, had found the hotel's circuit breaker and was deliberately dimming the lights.

Like any good practical joker, Fotiu learned about his teammates' foibles and then would exploit them. A case in point was Nicky's teammate, John Davidson, who had a special sensitivity to finding lobsters in his bed; usually too late.

At one hotel during a Rangers road trip, Fotiu discovered that there was sea food restaurant near the lobby and it featured a large tank filled with live lobsters. Nicky made a note of that and then patiently waited til Davidson fell asleep in his room.

Fotiu tiptoed out of the room, went directly to the restaurant and purchased a live lobster. He then caught the elevator and returned to find Davidson snoring vibrantly. With that, Nicky deftly pulled back the blanket and sheets and deposited the lobster an inch from Davidson's left thigh.

"I watched the lobster crawl out of the sheets and right up to Davidson's nose," Fotiu remembered. "John was sleeping through all this but when it crawled over his face, he woke up and let out a scream like a Banshee."

Bill Goldsworthy, Nick's roomate, was also victimized by the very same Fotiu. His ploy was disguising himself as his teammate's suit.

"While Goldie was dressing," said Nick, "I sneaked into the closet and climbed under the plastic covering over Bill's suit. In the dark it was impossible to tell that I was there."

After completing his morning wash-up-brush-teeth ritual, Goldsworthy decided to have breakfast. He walked to the closet, lifted the clothes hanger and took it out of the closet, not knowing that Nicky was underneath.

"When he opened the zipper and saw me there he nearly fainted," Fotiu chuckled.

The act of giving a friend a hot-foot is as old as hockey itself but dishing out hot SEATS is a relatively new form of practical jokery which Fotiu refined while still a Rangers. Naturally, Ferguson was the victim.

Fergie was intently watching his team hold a scrimmage at Madison Square Garden. The general manager's concentration was so intense that he was unaware that a six-foot, two hundred pound hulk had crawled under the loge seats armed with a rolled up newspaper. Fotiu stuffed the paper under Ferguson's seat, put a lit match to it and then stealthily crawled away.

"Instead of getting a hot foot," said Ferguson, "I wound up with a hot seat."

Chapter Six

LEAKY BOATES, LEGS FRASER AND HOCKEY'S MOST MEMORABLE PLAYOFF WAR

There have been hockey rivalries and there have been hockey *rivalries* but the competition between the Canadian Maritime cities of Sydney and Glace Bay in 1941 could only be described as out and out warfare. And even that may be an understatement. To this day old timers in Nova Scotia still talk about "The Legs Fraser Incident" as if it happened yesterday.

Yet through the whole ugly playoff mess that rocked the steel city of Sydney and the coal town that was Glace Bay there also were enough riotously funny sideshows to keep reporters in stitches long after the last goal was scored.

For that we can eternally thank such characters as Marty McDonald, manager of the Glace Bay Miners, of whom Reader's Digest author David MacDonald once noted, "his tangled intrigues owed less to Conn Smythe than to Niccolo Machiavelli.

McDonald was ably abetted by a tall, mean-spirited goaltender named Bill (Legs) Fraser, who often used his goalie stick as a scythe rather than to stop pucks which, incidentally, he did better than most in his trade. Not to mention Ernie Boates, another goaltender who was nicknamed Leaky with exquisite precision.

Under normal conditions, the paths of Legs Fraser and Leaky Boates would not have crossed during those early World War II years. Ah, but those were not "normal conditions" that spring when playoff fever gripped Nova Scotia.

So, a brief explanation: there were three teams in the Cape Breton League and of the trio, Glace Bay Miners and Sydney Millionaires were neck-and-neck as the best. The North Sydney Victorias were a poor third — except for one thing. They boasted Legs Fraser who just happened to be one of Canada's best goaltenders, NHL or otherwise.

This normally wouldn't have mattered since Fraser's Victorias were eliminated from the playoffs and he was not on either the Miners' nor Millionaires' roster. Meanwhile, the cities of Glace Bay and Sydney girded for the playoffs in a manner that might have been more appropriate for Paris and Berlin in August 1914.

The hockey hatred that prevailed between the Maritime metropoli in those days is easily explained when one considers the diverse nature of the two realms. The patrician Sydney, with a population of 25,000 was a steel city dominated by the power Dominion Steel and Coal Corporation. To the good folks of Glace Bay, DOSCO, as David MacDonald noted, "owned the collieries and controlled their lives." The coal center sent some 3,000 miners down under the Atlantic every day to toil in the pits.

To grimy Glace Bay, Sydney, only 13 miles away, was what Manhattan's Upper East Side is to the South Bronx, a place to be envied. However, one way to even the score was on the ice and in 1941 Marty MacDonald, all of 33 years old, had put together a nifty team.

How he did this is a story in itself since the wily MacDonald, like others in the Cape Breton League, was supposed to sprinkle only four "imports" on his roster. Since nobody told Marty "positively only four," the Miners managed ten out-of-towners. A grade-school drop-out, MacDonald, in his fractured English, rationalized that his club was entitled because of "the old rivalry."

Sydney was pushed down to second place in "the old

rivaltry" thanks, in part, to the adroit Glace Bay player-coach Jo-Jo Graboski and two other imports, goalie Jimmy Foster and forward Moe White.

Glace Bay supporters to this day will argue that there was a plot to torpedo their team and that Sydney people would do anything to ensure that the Millionaires would eventually prevail. Sure enough, word had begun filtering up and down the Canadian Amateur Hockey Association grapevine that the transfer papers belonging to White and Foster were not quite kosher. Matter of fact, Foster's branch transfer disappeared. As for White, he ostensibly worked for a Quebec firm that had "sent" him to Glace Bay on business. However, upon examination, the Quebec company denied any knowledge of a Moe White.

Having checked out both White's and Foster's credentials, the CAHA on February 11, 1941, dropped its bomb on Glace Bay. Both players were suspended for the rest of the season and the playoffs.

Enter Ernie Boates.

Marty MacDonald inserted the 19-year-old substitute goalie into Foster's crease and hoped that he would stop the oncoming Millionaires. Alas, Boates allowed five goals, Sydney moved into first and Ernie was forever known as Leaky Boates from that moment on.

According to David MacDonald, (no relation) who chronicled the season, Marty MacDonald was so nervous about Boates he was beside himself. After all, how could Glace Bay possibly beat Sydney with Leaky between the pipes?

David MacDonald: "Though the lad improved in the next outing, Marty MacDonald was not reassured. Looking ahead to facing Sydney in the playoff series — in his parlance, "a series with all the old rivaltry" — the Miners' manager knew they could never win with Leaky Boates in goal.

"Now, in dealing with earlier problems, Marty had displayed an eye for angles Euclid never knew. Once, concerned about a high scorer handicapped by monumental hangovers, he even persuaded the police to keep him in protective custody before a crucial game."

But what could the wily MacDonald possibly do to save his goaltending and his team this time? Ernie Boates was, well, Leaky, to say the least.

Eureka! Marty had the answer. Granted, it was all on the up and up but, what the hell, that made MacDonald even happier. Checking the CAHA fine print, Marty discovered that because of the war he was permitted to replace any player who happened to enlist in the armed forces.

Next, he grabbed Ernie Boates and slapped 200 dollar bills in the lad's hand. "This is your's if you enlist right now!"

But Leaky made it clear to his manager that he'd much rather face rubber than bullets. "Okay," said MacDonald, "here's $100, buy yourself a train ticket to Montreal and stay there until you hear from me."

Boates took the money and, as MacDonald had hoped, faded from view.

That done, Marty got on the phone with the CAHA and put out the word that his ONLY goaltender had disappeared. If the officials bought that cock-and-Boates story, it would mean that MacDonald could obtain a substitute goalie and why not the inimitable Legs Fraser.

All these delicious thoughts danced through Marty's head the next morning as he walked past Mrs. Russell MacPhee's boarding house which Ernle Boates had called home until, ostensibly, leaving for Montreal. MacDonald decided to drop in just to be sure his man HAD taken the money and ran.

Egad! In walked Marty and there sat Leaky on his bed. And what, pray tell, are you doing there rather than Montreal. As Boates simply replied, why should he go to Montreal, of all places, when he didn't know a soul there?

As luck would have it, before MacDonald could punch out Boates, through the window they noticed the approaching figure of hockey writer from a Sydney newspaper. If the scribe found Boates, all hell would break loose so Marty quickly urged his goalie to duck under the bed and stay there until the literary gumshoe disappeared.

Leaky obliged and stayed under the bed while MacDonald welcomed the reporter. "Where's Boates?" the newsmen demanded. Oh, Leaky, he's joined the Canadian Army was the manager's riposte. With that, the journalist departed and when MacDonald was certain that the scribe was far enough away, he invited Leaky to rejoin humanity on top rather than under the bed.

This time, MacDonald persuaded Boates that Montreal was a delightful place to visit, filled with cultural centers and other distinctly appealing sights. And to ensure that Leaky got the message, Marty personally escorted the goaltender to the railroad station, bought a ticket and put his man on the train heading west.

Now MacDonald's plot really began to thicken. He stuck a defenseman in goal for a meaningless final regular season game against North Sydney and then, supposedly, planned for the playoffs, a best-of-seven showdown with Sydney.

This had the Millionaires' officials licking their chops. Without Foster in goal for Glace Bay, Sydney would be the favorite and the gates from at least two — possibly four — home games would put them in the black.

Which is precisely what MacDonald was thinking when he announced at a league meeting on February 27th that his club was dropping out of playoff competition. Since he didn't have a goalie, Marty explained, it was pointless to go on and that was that.

No, that wasn't that, the Sydney officials shot back. They desperately wanted the playoffs to go on for artistic and fiscal reasons. Their solution; allow Legs Fraser to play goal for Glace Bay. It was an offer MacDonald couldn't refuse; mostly because it was the offer he had been hoping for all along.

While some Sydney supporters questioned the generosity, management believed that their club was too talented to lose, even if Fraser was the Glace Bay goalie.

Clearly, they were in error. One-two-three, Legs led the Miners to consecutive victories and within one win of the Maritime championship. The municipality of Glace Bay prepared for a celebration to end all hockey celebrations. And well they deserved it, they figured, if the series would end in four straight victories.

Across the city line there were forebodings of disaster and demands that immediate moves be taken to avoid a fourth defeat. But how? Millionaires officials went directly to the so-called source of the problem, the CAHA, and urged that Legs Fraser be a). disqualified from the tournament and, b). all of the Miners' wins with Fraser in goal be erased.

When news of the counter-ploy reached Glace Bay, its citizens reacted with more than outrage; they were ready to go to war with their sister-city and war means, you-know-what, sanctions. Real, no-holds-barred embargoes.

The first blow was struck by the Glace Bay merchants who agreed to boycott all Sydney wholesalers and retail stores until Legs Fraser was returned to the nets for the Miners. But Sydneyites were not through. Judge A.D. Campbell of Sydney, who happened to be president of the Cape Breton League, ruled that all three Glace Bay wins were invalid and, no, there would be no Fraser named Legs playing any more goal for the Miners. And that was that!

The war got worse. Barricades were erected at the city line preventing Sydney delivery trucks access to Glace Bay. If a Sydney citizen happened to be in Glace Bay, he or she was refused service in the Glace Bay restaurant. "One Glace Bay priest invoked divine aid," said David MacDonald.

Then the war got even worse. Glace Bay had one element economically dear to Sydney and that was coal. It suddenly became a weapon when Glace Bay mayor Dan Willie Morrision, who happened to be president of the district's United Mine Workers, sent a telegram to the CAHA. "FEAR THERE MAY BE STOPPAGE OF WORK IN MINES. FEAR THIS MAY RESULT IN STOPPAGE OF COAL SHIPMENT TO SYDNEY."

While it may sound funny more than a half-century later, the idea that hundreds of coal miners would walk out because of a hockey game was not amusing to residents of Sydney. A headline in the local paper warned, "MAY STOP WORK IN PITS AS PROTEST IN HOCKEY BATTLE."

The series' fourth game was slated for March 10 in Glace Bay but before it erupted a number of events changed the course of hockey history. Leaky Boates, who was supposed to be enjoying the Montreal scene, was discovered by a Sydney citizen in Truro, Nova Scotia and, no, he was not in the Canadian Army!

Boates quickly phoned MacDonald and told his ex-boss that the handwriting was on the wall. What to do? "Come on back," barked MacDonald, "and bring my money!"

Ernie obliged and was told that he'd be starting Game Four which now was really Game One since the first three wins had been disqualified. There were 5,000 spectators in Glace Bay Arena hoping for a miracle from Boates but, alas, Ernle was never more true to his nickname and when the final buzzer was sounded fish covered the ice to symbolize Leaky's 9-1 defeat.

That was enough for MacDonald. He forfeited the rest of the series, enabling Sydney to advance to the Allan Cup finals where they lost to Regina Pats.

As for Boates, this time he really joined the army along with Moe White, one of the two imports who started the uprising. Both returned from World War II and settled in Montreal, of all places, where Leaky managed a textile plant.

Amazingly, nobody ever coaxed the true story of his disappearance out of Boates although just about everyone connected with Maritime hockey presumed that crafty Marty MacDonald had masterminded the move. When last contacted, MacDonald would only say that he was responsible for a truly zany chapter in Canadian hockey history. Who can argue with the man when he concludes, "I made it a *serious* to remember!"

Seriously.

Chapter Seven

INCREDIBLE BUT TRUE (... MOSTLY...)

The Case of the Telltale Stick

Under Scotty Bowman's coaching regime in Montreal, the Canadiens won four straight Stanley Cups between 1976 and 1979.

A key to Bowman's success was his disciplinary tactics, which the Habs learned the hard way on a West Coast jaunt.

Montreal had beaten the Kings at The Forum in Inglewood, California and were looking forward to celebrating with a night on the town in Los Angeles.

Although there was no game scheduled the next day, Bowman imposed a curfew on the club and several players were vexed over Scotty's decision.

Feeling unjustly confined, a group of players took off for the bright lights and watering holes.

Many hours later — long after the curfew — the entourage returned to the hotel only to be greeted by an enthusiastic doorman who seemed like an avid hockey fan.

Armed with an authentic Canadiens' hockey stick, the doorman asked each of the incoming players if they would be good enough to autograph his stick. Feeling no pain, the Habs were glad to oblige and each put his John Hancock on the stick shaft.

Little did they realize that their signatures would incriminate them.

At breakfast the next morning, Bowman singled out every one of the curfew-breakers and doled out fines.

How did Bowman know which players were guilty?

Simple. It was the coach who had given the stick to the doorman, asking him to get the post-Midnight players to sign their names — and inadvertently admit their guilt.

The Forgotten Bonus That Almost Inspired Gordie Howe to Stay Out of Hockey

As a teenager, Gordie Howe was invited to the Detroit Red Wings training camp. Red Wings manager Jack Adams was impressed with Howe and decided that he would sign him to a contract. The pair discussed the financial arrangement and shook hands on a deal.

"Gordie was quite reasonable about everything," said Adams, "but he insisted on one extra; he wanted a windbreaker jacket decorated with his team's insignia. Of course I agreed to that modest request. Then, in a press of more important business, I forgot all about it.

"After Gordie spent a winter working out, I decided at the following training camp to have him turn pro for our farm club at Omaha in the United States Hockey League. Howe appeared to like the pro terms I outlined to him, but seemed loath to sign the contract.

"I sensed that something was wrong but couldn't imagine what it could be so I spoke up. 'What seems to be the matter, Gordie? Why the hesitation about signing? You like the contract, don't you?'

"The boy just about floored me when he answered glumly, 'The salary is all right, but what about that windbreaker you promised me when I signed last year's contract?'"

According to Adams that was the first and last argument he had with Gordie Howe. The windbreaker was delivered, as promised, and Howe ultimately emerged as hockey's greatest star, playing for Jack Adams' Red Wings.

Paying For No Pay

Can you believe that a hockey star once refused payment for participating in a Stanley Cup game?

Yes, it did happen.

Eddie Gerard played for the Toronto St. Patrick's in one game of the 1922 Stanley Cup finals between Vancouver and Toronto. Originally a member of the Ottawa Senators, Gerard was asked to dress for Toronto in the Cup finals after St. Patrick's ace defenceman Harry Cameron took sick. Vancouver boss Lester Patrick approved the use of Gerard. At the time it appeared that Vancouver would win the series but Toronto tied it at two games apiece by winning game four, 6-0. The one sided defeat of his skaters frightened Patrick, who now refused to permit Gerard to play the fifth and deciding game of the series. When Cameron got word of that he climbed out of his sick bed and rejoined his teammates as they routed Vancouver, 5-1.

Charlie Querrie, owner of the Cup-winning Torontonians singled out Eddie Gerard who had played so capably when he substituted for Cameron in the fourth game, which tilted the series towards the St. Pats. "You were great, just great," said Querrie. "What do you think I should pay you for playing for us?"

Gerard, a gentleman from the old school, shook his head and grinned. "Forget it. I don't want a penny. This was as much fun as I've had all year!"

Reluctantly, Querrie obliged Gerard, but, nevertheless, ordered a diamond ring for Eddie and thanked him profusely for grand play, and sportsmanlike attitude.

Of Superstition and Religion

Few big-league hockey players would dare admit that they have no superstitions, but some skaters are more superstitious than others. Ever since he broke into the bigs with the Chicago Black Hawks, centre Phil Esposito has been notarized for his collection of good luck charms. When Esposito played for the Boston Bruins, he shared locker room facilities with Derek Sanderson, who was conspicuously less superstitious than Espo. As a result, Sanderson was called upon to aid and abet Phil.

"From the beginning," said Sanderson, "I had to put up with Phil's superstitions. I would fix his shoulder pads just right; put on his suspenders and all that. I'd be on the floor doing my skates and Espie would say, "All right, do my shoulder pads." And I'd have no choice. I'd just have to do it and then go back to my skates. I'd say, `Jesus, Espie, what's the matter with you?" Right away he'd answer in his inimitable way, "I got a superstition, kid, a SUPER-STISH."

One of those superstitions involved wearing something black under his Bruins' jersey; a dickey with a high neck. "It just slips over my head," said Phil, "and down over my chest. I wore it one night against Toronto because I had a cold. Got three goals that night, so I wore it ever since. I dress right to left. I put my right sock on first, then my left. Then everything else, right first, then the left. And we go out on the ice the same way all the time."

Esposito's longtime foe during the late 1960's and 1970's was Montreal Canadiens' left winger John Ferguson. Like Esposito, Fergie had his share of good luck ploys and plans. One Sunday morning when the Canadiens and New York Rangers were engaged in a Stanley Cup playoff round, Ferguson was strolling across West 49th street in Manhattan when he came upon *Montreal Star* columnist Pat Curran, who was enroute to the Actor's Chapel of St. Malachy's Church near the old Madison Square Garden. When Curran told Ferguson where he was going, Fergie put his hand in his pocket and pulled out a quarter. "Here," said the Canadiens' winger, "light a candle for me." That same night, Ferguson scored the winning goal in sudden death overtime, winning the series for Montreal.

As any coach, player or manager will admit, prayers

don't always work. Emile Francis, one time boss of the St. Louis Blues, once played goal for the Chicago Black Hawks and made a number of friends in the Windy City. One of them was a Monsignor. When the Francis-coached New York Rangers reached the seventh game of a playoff against the Black Hawks years later, the Monsignor came along to say Sunday mass in Francis' suite in the Hotel Bismarck.

It didn't work; the Rangers played their worst game of the series and the Black Hawks moved on to the finals.

On the other hand, Francis remembered the power of the prayer working for him when he was coaching in Guelph, Ontario and his Junior team was playing the powerful Toronto St. Michael's team.

"We haven't got a chance," muttered one of Francis' players. "I just saw the whole St. Michael's team coming out of church.

"I've got some news for you," said Francis. "I was in that same church praying just as hard as they were."

That night Francis' team won.

George ("Punch") Imlach, who orchestrated the Toronto Maple Leafs, had been among the most superstitious of hockey people ever since he played for the old Quebec Aces of the Quebec Senior Hockey League. During one series he bought a new suit each time he brought the Maple Leafs to the Montreal Forum.

"Will it help?" someone asked Punch.

"Sure," Imlach replied, "if my goalie is good and we score a lot of goals!"

How an NHL Club Won and Lost the Stanley Cup on the Same Day!

The 1924 Montreal Canadiens had defeated Ottawa, Vancouver and Calgary in the playoffs to capture the ice title and, as a tribute to the winners, the citizens of Montreal hailed the Cup kings with a public reception.

The Cup was officially presented to the Canadiens and all players received momentos from the University of Montreal. (It was the only time in history that a professional hockey team had been so honored by a major learning institution.) Following the reception, the Canadiens repaired to the home of club owner Leo Dandurand for an informal get-together. Goalie Georges Vezina, Sprague Cleghorn, Sylvio Mantha and Dandurand climbed into a Model-T Ford to make the trip.

Climbing the Cote St. Antoine Road hill in Westmount, the Ford stalled and all the occupants but the driver, climbed out to give it a push. That's when the Cup-winners became Cup-losers. Dandurand recalled the episode as follows:

"Cleghorn, who had been jealously carrying the hard-won Stanley Cup in his lap, deposited it on the curb at the roadside before he joined us in shoving the car up the hill. When we reached the top, we hopped back into the car and resumed our hockey chatter as we got going again. Upon reaching my house, we all started in on a big bowl of punch which my wife he prepared. It wasn't until she asked, `Well where is this Stanley Cup you've been talking about?' that we realized that Cleghorn had left it on the side of the road. Sprague and I drove hurriedly back to the spot almost an hour after we had pushed the car up the hill. There was the Cup in all its shining majesty, still sitting on the curb of the busy street."

Best Put Down of a Defense Prospect
When Tom Webster coached the Los Angeles Kings during the 1991-92 season, he was asked about a spectacular goal scored by Rob Blake against Edmonton.

"He looked like Bobby Orr on that one," snapped Webster. "Some nights, however, he looks like iron ore!"

The Guy Who Couldn't Shoot the Puck in the Ocean
You've heard the expression dozens of times: "That no good so-and-so is such a bum forward he couldn't shoot the puck into the ocean if he was standing on the shore."

But how many times has a victim of such a devastating hockey insult been able to prove — or disprove — the theory?

Well, once it actually happened.

The player in question was a Detroit Red Wings forward named Rene Fernand Gauthier, a native of Chicoutimi, Quebec (home town of the immortal Georges Vezina). Gauthier had actually played some pretty good hockey during the World War II years with both the New York Rangers and Montreal Canadiens. But now the war had ended and the quality of the National hockey league game experienced a steady rise. Concomitantly, Gauthier's game experienced an equally steady decline.

The more he skated for the motor city sextet, the more difficult it was to imagine that he had once scored 14 goals for the Rangers and 18 for the Canadiens in a season. As a Red Wing, he was getting zilch.

In his first season with Detroit he scored nine times and added three more in the playoffs. But a year after that he managed only one and the year after that only one again.

The less Gauthier scored, the more needling he absorbed and the less ice time he was given. He was reduced to penalty killing — he was outstanding in that role — but he soon earned the label from his mates as the player who "couldn't put a puck in the ocean."

At the time Stan Saplin was the publicity director of the Rangers and picked up on the Gauthier gag. "In no time at all," said Saplin, "the gag had spread around the league, but Fern took it good naturedly."

Another who heard the puck in ocean routine was Lew Walter, hockey writer for the Detroit Times. Eventually, the paths of Walter, Saplin and Gauthier would cross, thereby creating a mini hockey legend.

"Lew got to thinking about all the ribbing," Saplin recalled, "but he realized it was unfair, in Detroit, to say that Fern couldn't put the puck in the ocean since Detroit was hundreds and hundreds of miles from such a body of water.

"One morning, though, when the Red Wings checked into a New York hotel, prior to a game with the Rangers, Walter picked up a phone and arranged for a photographer to meet him. Then he phoned Gauthier and gave him certain instructions."

Saplin was informed of the grand scheme as were a few New York writers. "Within an hour, Walter, the photographer, and Gauthier, carrying a hockey stick and a handful of pucks, were on their way downtown. They headed for the Battery, at the tip of Manhattan island, and there, with the photographer getting the evidence on film to disprove, once and for all, the false legend."

Just to be sure the evidence was well-weighted on Gauthier's side, a number of Detroit players were invited along to act as additional witnesses.

"We took along Gordie Howe, Ted Lindsay, and Marty

Pavelich," said Walter. "They were able to refute the first two supposed 'misses' made by Gauthier."

One version had it that Gauthier missed on his first two attempts. "It was said," Walter laughed, "that as Fern shot the first puck a sea gull swooped down and snatched it -- and then as the second puck went sailing out, a tugboat came by chuffing with a string of barges, on one of which the puck landed."

Both Saplin and Walter insist that Fern was able to shoot the puck into the Atlantic Ocean.

"Fern proved," Walter concluded, "not only that he could put the puck in the ocean, but also that he was a good sport by entering into the spirit of the rib. He was a winger of great potential, of fine personality, and, if injuries had not hampered him, might have made him a true success in professional hockey!"

If nothing else, he will be remembered for his non-scoring; certainly a first in hockey.

North Stars Won is a Loser

Minnesota North Stars owner Norman Green thought he was doing his players a favor when he bought a Douglas DC-9 as the team plane. The aircraft was promptly named North Stars Won but it turned out to be a loser.

The main purpose of a team plane is to avoid long delays that plague winter travelers. Unfortunately, North Stars Won was no help.

A two hour trip from Calgary to San Francisco wound up taking seven hours.

On Halloween Night 1991 the club had a real nightmare. Following a game in Pittsburgh, North Stars Won was stuck on the runway until 3 a.m. until the players finally debarked and stayed at a hotel. The next morning they were still delayed and didn't arrive home until 3 p.m. some 24 hours after the game.

Before the next trip, North Stars Won was grounded because of engine problems.

With that, Green issued the order: LOSE NORTH STARS WON.

From then on they travelled by commercial airlines.

Detroit's Octopus Pitcher

Hockey fans have been among the most creative in sports, but there has never been any to match a denizen of Detroit's old Olympia Stadium, because he was an octopus pitcher! The fellow's name was Pete Cusimano.

Mankind is grimly returning to the ape state, but the determined march is sometimes relieved by rare cashews like Pete, who are unafraid to act, as the charming colloquialism goes, a little milky in the filbert. Pete's surname was Cusimano — the swarthy, stocky scion of an old Sicilian family, in the coffee-selling game in Detroit. His peculiar avocation was pitching octopi into hockey rinks — mostly in the old Detroit Olympia Stadium.

It was during the 1952 playoffs when the first octopus was pitched from the stands. Detroit was looking to capture the Stanley Cup in just eight games, having swept the semifinals in four straight and currently leading the Montreal Canadiens in the finals, three games to none. Enter the Cusimano family from the bullpen.

"My dad was also in the fish and poultry business," Pete later told interviewers. "My brother Jerry and me helped him, and often after work, we'd go to the Red Wing games." With Detroit in perfect position to sweep the playoffs in eight straight, Jerry came up with a new good luck charm before the eighth game. He suggested to Pete: "Why don't we throw an octopus on the ice for good luck? It's got eight legs, and that might be a good omen for eight straight wins."

So, on April 15, 1952, Jerry Cusimano went into his wind up and the first octopus was pitched in the Detroit Olympia. Referee Frank Udvari was one of the many unsuspecting people that night. "You should have seen how Udvari jumped when he saw our first octopus!" recollected Pete.

The Canadiens didn't stand a chance against this omen. They lost, 3-0, and the Red Wings had their eighth triumph in as many playoff games, as well as the Stanley Cup.

Tragically, Jerry Cusimano was killed in a car crash not long after hurling the first octopus, but brother Pete kept up the tradition for many seasons. Pete Cusimano kept his arm loose for whenever Detroit had a playoff crisis and threw many an octopus over those years.

The "stuff" Pete used on his pitches was quite simple. The octopi weighed in at around three pounds and were very sticky after being boiled into a deep crimson. "They don't exactly come up smelling like cherry custard," he testified. One time he grabbed a startled reporter and asked, "You ever smelt a half-boiled octopus? It ain't exactly channel No. 5, y'know."

A question always asked by reporters was about the pitching motion used by Cusimano and he would stand up to demonstrate. "You grip the thing in the palm of your hand," he explained. "You pick out your target. Then you rear back and heave it like you would a hand grenade. You got to keep your elbow stiff to get the best distance."

When asked if he ever picked out any special targets, he replied, "I look on the whole ice surface as my strike zone. But one time I got hot at Ted Kennedy of Toronto. He'd been having a big series against the Wings. Scoring a lot of goals and scragging a lot of our guys. So during a beef when they're all standing around arguing, I decide to let him have it." Pause. "Only I hit another Toronto player, Vic Lynn, who was standing right next to Kennedy, splat in the kisser."

Cusimano became a celebrity at Detroit and one night he was sitting near a priest and his friend.

"Psst, Father," the friend whispered. "You're sitting close to the celebrated octopus pitcher."

"Oh, no!" replied the clergyman, amazed.

Sure enough, Cusimano let fly during the game at referee Bill Friday, narrowly missing him.

"I'd have hit him, Father," Cusimano said, "If you'd have blessed the octopus."

Strange Objects on the Ice

Over the years, many weird objects have hit the ice during hockey games, especially during the playoffs.

Some of them were human, like the male streaker who vaulted the boards at Maple Leaf Gardens one night and made a run for the Leaf bench. Another night, in Los Angeles, three curvaceous ladies pranced from goal line to goal line clad only in their birthday suits.

Coins, programs and rotten eggs seem to be the most common items hurled by disgruntled fans. At the Los Angeles Forum one night, a Kings' fan tossed a live chicken, dressed in the home team purple and gold, over the boards.

A Detroit playoff series simply wouldn't be complete without a squid or an octopus making its annual appearance. Former NHL referee Red Storey says, "there's nothing as ugly or as slimy as one of those things on the ice. I'd always order a linesman or an arena worker to clean up the mess. I never wanted to touch one of those things myself!"

In Quebec City several years ago, three pigs, squealing in fright and dismay, were turned loose on the ice surface.

At the Montreal Forum in an era when it was customary to protect good shoe leather in winter, fans celebrated a big goal by the Rocket, Boom Boom or Big Jean by throwing their toe rubbers on the ice. Former Chicago Black Hawk winger Dennis Hull likes to tell about the time his father took him aside before a big game at the Forum. Anticipating a fatherly pep talk, Dennis was surprised to hear his father say, "Son, when the Habs score tonight and the rubbers hit the ice, grab me a good pair, will you? Size ten."

Pigeons, Bats and Other Fauna

Since many hockey teams are named after animals, it should not be surprising that some of our fine, feathered friends frequently inhabit NHL arenas.

Pigeons occupied the rafters of the old Madison Square Garden on Eighth Avenue in New York. When the ice was being resurfaced between periods, they would swoop down and drink from the puddles of water before the surface became completely frozen. However, the pigeons didn't make the trip downtown to the new Garden with the Rangers when it was opened in 1968.

When the Penguins joined the NHL in 1967 they bought a mascot, a live penguin named Pete. Trainers tried to teach him how to skate and just as Pete was making great strides, he died — of pneumonia.

During the 1975 Stanley Cup finals between the Flyers and Sabres, a bat invaded Buffalo's War Memorial Auditorium. Sabre forward Jim Lorentz became involved with the flying rodent, killing it with his stick.

"This thing came down," said Lorentz, "and began flying around a couple of feet above the ice. I don't know whether the bat was brought into the building in a paper sack and let loose or whether it lived there.

"The bat showed up ten minutes into the first period. Our goalie, Gerry Desjardins, took a swing at it with his goalie stick and missed. I took my swing during a face-off. We were down 2-0 at the time. Maybe that had something to do with it. The bat didn't help its own cause either, because rather than fluttering around like most bats, it flew in a straight line — sick maybe, or suicidal. It fell in front of Rick MacLeish. No one else wanted anything to do with it. But he took it over to the penalty box — and in his bare hand, what's more."

Then there was the Hall of Famer who was mistaken for a bear. That would be Rod Gilbert (pronounced Zhilbear) who starred for the Rangers in the 1960's and 1970's. One day during the prime of his career, Gilbert received a

letter from a young fan. The envelope read, ROGER BEAR.
Rod Gilbert, Roger Bear — close!

Disrobing the Stanley Cup

Some players say the greatest thing that ever happened to
them in hockey was winning The Stanley Cup. Phil Bourque
of the Pittsburgh Penguins is one of them — but then he
went one better, and took The Cup apart.

It happened in the spring of 1991 after the Penguins
had defeated the Minnesota North Stars in the playoff
finals. Like most of the Pittsburgh players, Bourque was
allowed to take the silverware to his home.

"I noticed that there was a loose nut on the inside of the
Cup," says Bourque, "and I decided that I couldn't give it
back like that. So, I took out my tool box and found out
that the bottom of the Cup comes off easy. It's a loose fit
but as you work your way up, way up toward the original
Cup, you see inside that some guys have etched their own
names. They've written in there, 'Repaired by...' and you
see all those French names, like Jacques Laperriere and
whatnot. I thought it was only fitting that I assume my
place among the repairmen."

Baun Scores the Winner on a Broken Leg!!!

Former Leaf stalwart Bobby Baun doesn't play old-timers'
hockey with us anymore — his doctor advised against it.
But Baun left many a memory, especially during the 1960's
when he teamed with Carl Brewer. We miss the man who
is often asked about his biggest moment in hockey. That
was the time he scored a winning playoff goal while skating on a broken leg - *A BROKEN LEG!!!*

Baun's memorable moment came in the sixth game of
the final series between the Leafs and the Red Wings. If the
Wings won, they would capture the Stanley Cup. With the
score tied 3-3, Gordie Howe of the Wings rifled a shot that

caught Baun just above the ankle. The Leaf d-man had to be carried off on a stretcher.

In the dressing room, Baun had a local anesthetic injected in the ankle to kill the pain, and when the game went into overtime, there he was back on the ice.

After one minute and 43 seconds of overtime, Baun took a pass from Bob Pulford and slapped the puck at Red Wings goaltender Terry Sawchuk. The disk deflected off Detroit defenseman Bill Gadsby and found the net for the winning goal. In 55 previous playoff games, Baun had scored only twice.

So it was back to Toronto for the seventh and deciding game. Baun disregarded doctors' advice to have his aching leg x-rayed. "Later," he said, "I'll do it later. Look after Kelly, Brewer and Mahovlich first." Leaf center Red Kelly was nursing sprained ligaments in his knee, defenseman Brewer had a rib separation, and left winger Frank Mahovlich had a bruised shoulder.

For the final game, Baun's leg had to be injected with the pain killer once again. He played a regular shift despite severe pain. It wasn't until the Leafs won the game 4-0 and had the Stanley Cup firmly in their grasp that he consented to have his leg x-rayed. The medical technicians confirmed what Baun had already suspected. A cast would be needed for the leg he'd broken a couple of nights earlier.

She Played for the New York Rangers, Brooklyn Dodgers and New York Knickerbockers

Gladys Goodding played at Rangers home hockey games, Knickerbockers basketball games (both in Madison Square Garden) and Dodgers baseball games at Ebbetts Field in the 1940's and 1950's. She played organ.

At National Hockey League games, Miss Goodding would play different songs for the various NHL teams: "Canadian Capers" for Montreal; "Pretty Red Wing" for Detroit; "Chicago" for the Black Hawks and "The Ranger Victory Song" for the home team.

For reasons never explained, Miss Goodding invariably banged out a tune called "Saskatchewan" when the Maple Leafs took the ice although Toronto's sextet is very much a part of Ontario. Never did she try "Maple Leaf Rag," composed by the immortal Scott Joplin.

Why Wait for the Opening Whistle?

It happened in the spring of 1987, in the Stanley Cup Playoffs, and it brought shame to the National Hockey League. It was a playoff "first," and it caused the start of the sixth game to be delayed 15 minutes in the Wales Conference Finals between the Flyers and the Canadiens.

What was it? It was an incredible 10-minute brawl between Philly and Montreal, and it happened before the game even started.

The brawl was sparked by a silly superstition, nothing more, nothing less. Some of the Montreal Canadiens, for some reason that remains unknown, had developed a habit of shooting a puck into the opposing team's empty net at the end of the pre-game warm up. They did it when most of the players had left the ice. Few people noticed, and few people cared. It was just a silly superstition.

But this night, when Shane Corson and Claude Lemieux slipped the puck into the Flyer net at the end of the warm-up period, out stormed Philly tough guy Ed Hodospar. He was incensed that the Habs would invade the flyer end of the rink — even in the warm up period — and he attacked Lemieux.

That did it. Players from both clubs jumped back on the ice and a major brawl ensued. Forum fans had never seen anything like it. The next day reporters called it "disgusting," "appalling," and "shameful."

The two teams were fined more than $24,000 each, and Hodospar was suspended for the balance of the playoffs as the instigator of the ugly brawl. He explained his attack on Lemieux by saying, "If it was that important to him, then it was important to me. Everyone is looking for a little edge in the playoffs."

It was the low point of thew playoffs, and all because of a ridiculous superstition.

The Fox is Fooled
When Bill Dineen played for the Detroit Red Wings, he earned the nickname "The Fox" by ignoring curfew and by slyly allowing others to take credit for his success.

He looks like a professor but has acted otherwise. Once, in Houston, he ran into the stands to attack the irksome owner of the opposition and his players followed him. He once jumped into a swimming pool in a tuxedo and his team followed him there as well.

Few people pull a fast one on Dineen but one who did was his first manager, Jack (Jolly Jawn) Adams, who ran the Red Wings when Dineen arrived at training camp in 1953-54. For his first season, Bill was paid $6,000 and had such a good season that Adams invited him into his office before the 1954-55 campaign began.

"You did everything we asked of you," said Adams. "You scored, you checked, you played head's up hockey. Young man, I'm going to give you a $500 raise."

Tickled with the increase, Dineen gladly inked the new pact and then headed for the dressing room where his teammates were meeting. It was only then that Dineen learned that during the summer, NHL owners had raised the NHL minimum salary from $6,000 to $6,500.

Bill Dineen's Unclean Victory Parade
Former NHL and WHA forward Rich Preston swears that this actually happened when he played for the Houston Aeros.

"Bill Dineen was our coach when we won the Avco World Cup, which was the WHA's version of the Stanley

Cup," says Preston. "The Avco Cup was quite a big deal to the Houston people and they arranged a victory parade for us.

"As it happened, the arrival of the circus coincided with the Cup celebration. What they did was have some of the players ride on top of the elephants as well as our coach, Dineen.

"Everything was going along fine until the parade made a stop at a red light. Unfortunately, the elephant in front of Bill's elephant decided to take a large crap.

"Elephants being elephants, Bill's elephant gathered the big pile of shit in its curled trunk and then casually tossed it over its back. The dung landed right in Dineen's lap.

"And poor coach couldn't do a thing about it — til the parade ended a half-hour later!"

The Player in Green

Can you believe that a member of the Toronto Maple Leafs once played in an NHL game while dressed in a green uniform?

It happened on March 17, 1934 — St. Patrick's Day — and the man in green was that irrepressible Irishman, defenseman King Clancy.

Clancy threw aside his traditional blue and white uniform that night and donned a green jersey with a large white shamrock stitched to the back. It was his night — King Clancy Night at the Gardens — and there's never been a night quite like it.

Before the game, a number of colorful floats were wheeled onto the ice surface. Out of a large potato popped several junior players. Leaf star Harold Cotton emerged from a mammoth top hat. George Hainsworth, the goalie, was hidden in a boot, while Red Horner, the Leaf tough guy, fought his way out of a huge boxing glove.

Then, with the arena lights dimmed, Clancy, the King of hockey, entered the arena riding a float in the shape of a throne. He was wearing royal robes and a silver crown. Clancy's pals, Charlie Conacher and Hap Day, helped him down from his throne, and when he turned to thank them they impishly hurled coal dust in his face.

After receiving a grandfather clock and a silver tea service as mementos of the occasion, Clancy, his face still black and his uniform green, went to work against the Rangers.

But after one period, Ranger coach Lester Patrick had seen enough. He collared King and asked him to please change back to blue and white because his green shirt was confusing all of the Rangers' players.

Suspended for Life!
Over the years, many players have been suspended from hockey for various lengths of time. Only three times in NHL history have players received lifetime suspensions.

Back in 1927, during a playoff game between Boston and Ottawa, Bill Coutu — often known as Couture— of the Bruins assaulted referee Jerry Laflamme and knocked him down to the ice. He then proceeded to knock down linesman Bill Bell with a flying tackle.

All of this took place right in front of League President Frank Calder, who sentenced Coutu to a lifetime suspension and fined him $100. Teammates and opponents alike breathed easier with Coutu gone from the game. The ten year veteran had established himself as a mean tempered individual who would deliver as many crushing bodychecks in team scrimmages as he did in the games.

Five years later, Coutu's suspension was lifted, but by then he was too old to return to the NHL.

Two players banned from the game waited much longer to be reinstated. Compared to them, Coutu was lucky.

On March 9, 1947, NHL President Clarence Campbell sentenced Billy Taylor of the New York Rangers and Don Gallinger of the Boston Bruins to lifetime sentences away from the NHL after he discovered they were associating with gamblers and placing bets on NHL games. Gallinger admitted later that he bet up to $1,000 on the outcome of games, but that only a handful of games were involved. Campbell stressed that no fix of any game was involved or even attempted.

All efforts to have the pair reinstated, even long after their playing days were over, were rebuffed by Campbell and the NHL owners. The suspensions were not lifted until 1970, when both players were middle aged. Taylor returned to hockey as a coach and a scout, Gallinger did not. Their penalties were (and still remain) the most severe ever levied by an NHL president.

Shore Gets Even

Springfield Indians owner Eddie Shore ranks among the most tight-fisted of hockey bosses. During the late 1940's his top player, Mike Narduzzi, wanted a raise from his $3,700 a year salary.

Shore wouldn't budge and Narduzzi responded by holding out for the first month of the new season, demanding $4,500.

In time, Shore agreed to pay his ace. The two signed the new contract after which Shore fined Narduzzi $800 for reporting late.

Another fine player who had problems with Shore was center Bill Sweeney. A dandy stickhandler, Sweeney occasionally suffered weight problems of which Shore was acutely aware.

After a scrimmage one day, Shore walked into the dressing room, noticed the naked Sweeney and asked, "Sweeney, are you pregnant?"

The center mulled over the question for a few seconds and then replied, "Well, Eddie, considering the number of times you've raped me on my contract, I probably am!"

Unusual Names for Tom McVie's Children

Veteran coach Tom McVie supposedly named his two sons, Dallas and Denver, after cities in which he worked but the truth is somewhat different.

Dallas was named after a longtime NHL defenseman, Dallas Smith, who once was McVie's teammate. Denver got his monicker after a gunfighter in a Western that McVie watched on TV after his wife gave birth.

Hollywood and Hockey

John (Duke) Wayne, arguably the most popular actor in Hollywood history, portrayed a high-scoring forward in the 1937 film "Idol of the Crowds." Whether or not Wayne could skate was never known since he was never actually shown in full flight. In one sequence the camera zeroed in on his upper torso and in another down to a pair of skating legs.

Ryan O'Neal starred in "Love Story." He played a varsity stickhandler for Harvard's team. And Paul Newman amused theatergoers with his portrayal of a minor league player-coach in "Slapshot," directed by George Roy Hill. Unlike Wayne, Newman actually indulged in on-the-ice sequences.

A matinee idol in the 1930's, Louis Hayward portrayed a hockey-playing military cadet in the 1939 flick "The Duke of West Point." The highlight of the film was a match between the United States Military Academy team and the Royal Military College from Canada.

Dick Purcell, another heartthrob of the same era, was featured in "King of Hockey," which premiered in 1936. The co-star was Wayne Morris.

A few years later the Dead End Kids, led by Leo Gorcey and Huntz Hall, engaged in a hockey game as part of the script for "Hell's Kitchen" which was released in 1939. At one point in the movie the Dead Enders play a match against what they believe will be youngsters from another

school but turn out to be the "bad guys." Those "bad guys,"
according to some film critics, were played by members of
the New York Americans hockey club. Also in the cast was
a president-to-be named Ronald Reagan.

In 1973 Robert Mitchum teamed with Peter Boyle for
"The Friends of Eddie Coyle." Footage in the film was
taken at Boston Garden during an actual Bruin games.

Not surprisingly Canadian producers have come up
with full-length movies of their own. A 1971 production,
"Face Off," included National Hockey League stars Derek
Sanderson of the Boston Bruins and Jim McKenny of the
Toronto Maple Leafs. Former Maple Leafs right wing
George Armstrong also was in the movie.

Another Canadian feature followed three years later
when "Paperback Hero" made its debut. The backdrop
was Delisle, Saskatchewan, the wheat-growing town which
gained immortality for being the birthplace of Hall of
Famers Max and Doug Bentley. Keir Dullea starred in the
movie and Max Bentley enjoyed a cameo role.

Petty Cash
Decades ago, in the era before agents, attorneys and six
figure salaries for untried rookies, it was not uncommon
for big league managers to trim the budgets of their fresh-
men skaters to the bone. One of the tightest of these front
office types was William J. (Bill) Tobin, who managed the
Chicago Blackhawks in the late 1930's and 1940's.

"The expense account allowance," Tobin once explained,
"gave the boys a chance to imagine they were adult big
leaguers and they did some of the darndest things." Tobin
had figured he had seen everything until one day, a
youngster approached him on the fifth day of training
camp and said: "Mister Tobin, it's cost me a little extra
above the club's allowance to live here, and I'd like to get
something to cover my expenses."

Tobin expected a rather inflated figure and inquired how much the rookie had in mind.

"Just $10.35," he replied.

The unusual figure piqued Tobin's interest. "It's all right about the 10 dollars, but how do you figure the 35 cents?"

The youngster retorted with a perfectly straight face: "It'll cost me the 35 cents to send a telegram to my Dad to tell him about the 10 dollars!"

Because the Black Hawks were not selling out during the Depression days, Tobin was forced to be frugal beyond and above the call of duty. Once, he resorted to crawling on the ice to look for some front teeth that were lost by one of his players.

It happened in Chicago Stadium, when Hawks' defenceman Virgil Johnson ran up to Tobin in a state of shock and said, "Mister Tobin, I've lost my teeth. That bridgework in front was jarred loose in the last minute of play, and I can't find it on the ice."

Tobin had remembered how much the teeth had cost, and it was more than they could afford again. The manager asked Johnson to point out the spot where he believed the teeth had fallen, and they began searching. After eventually finding them, Tobin exclaimed, "I had saved the club a few precious bucks."

Like all fiscally sound managers, Tobin insisted that his players submit expense accounts for purchases made with the team's money. Among his favorites was one submitted by a rookie. It read as follows: "one sack of apples, one detective story magazine, one pair of shoelaces for his dress shoes; one box of small Epsom salts."

Tobin also suffered his share of contract disputes, but the most perplexing reply he ever received came from a sophomore who had completed a successful rookie season and demanded a hefty raise, far beyond Tobin's budget. The bickering went on for several weeks and finally caught the attention of the newspapers, whereupon the player dispatched the following wire to Tobin:

"DEAR BILL: SEE BY PAPERS I AM HOLDOUT. I AM NOT HOLDOUT BUT LIKE TO PLAY HOCKEY FOR YOU. HOWEVER I WILL NOT SIGN CONTRACT UNLESS I AM PAID MORE MONEY."

A Fine Thing

When Brett Hull of the St.Louis Blues was visiting the San Francisco Bay area with his club for a game against the San Jose Sharks, he hooked up with his Uncle Dennis Hull, who was with the Sharks broadcasting team.

Dennis was showing his nephew a good time when he suddenly looked at his watch and noticed that it was 12:45 a.m.

"I'd better get you back to the hotel," Dennis advised.

"What for?" asked Brett.

"Look at the time. What about your one o'clock curfew?"

"Don't worry about it."

"Why?"

Brett grinned knowingly. "The fines haven't caught up with the salaries yet. I'm making two million. The fine is $100."

A Fine Thing II

When Peter Mahovlich played for the Montreal Canadiens, he was renowned for his capers both on and off the ice, not to mention his chronic tardiness.

One night he returned to his hotel long after the curfew only to be met by coach Scotty Bowman.

"That'll cost you $100," snapped Bowman.

"Here's $200," Mahovlich replied. "The extra $100 pays for the next time I'm caught!"

The First Hockey Nickname

(Fred Taylor, born on June 23, 1883, in Tara, Ontario, became pro hockey's first superstar. He also was the first stickhandler to earn a nickname that stuck for life. Before his death, Taylor, in his own words, told me how he got the nickname Cyclone.)

"This all came about in 1907 after I'd been invited to play for Ottawa in a fine new arena which was distinguished not only for its size — it held about 7,000 people — but also because the Governor General of Canada, His Honor, Earl Grey, and members of Parliament liked to attend games there. In fact, the Governor General was at the opening of the rink in December 1907 when we played the Montreal Wanderers.

"The place was packed that night, because the Wanderers, the Stanley Cup champions, were a big attraction. Also, too, there was a fuss over the new arena and me.

"For this particular game I was moved back to defense instead of playing rover or a forward position. The Ottawa coach felt I could play defense, and the results made him look good. We beat Montreal, 8-5, and I scored five goals on individual rushes *(the method Bobby Orr supposedly "invented" 60 years later. — ed.)*

"One of the newspapermen covering that game was Malcolm Bryce, sports editor of the Ottawa Free Press. Hockey received big coverage in those days, and the Free Press was devoted to the game, about which Bryce wrote: 'I understand that this boy, Taylor, was nicknamed 'Tornado' when he played in Manitoba. And I further understand that when he moved into the International League they called him 'Whirlwind.' But starting today, based on his performance, last night, I am re-christening him 'Cyclone' Taylor.'

"That wasn't the only nickname I got. Once when we played an exhibition game in New York somebody called me "The Jim Jeffreys of the Ice" after the boxer. Naturally this made me feel great, because I was young at the time and very impressionable. But Cyclone fit best."

Eyes, a Bylaw and a Guy Named Trushinski

The toughest hockey question relevant to the NHL and eyesight goes like this: Who was Snoozer Trushinski?

For the answer you have to refer to the old NHL Bylaw 12.6 forbidding players who are sightless in one eye from playing in the league.

It states that players with one eye, or 3/60th of normal vision shall not be eligible to play for a member club. Loss of 75 percent of sight in an eye is required for insurance to take effect.

This regulation became known as "the Trushinski Bylaw" because of a player named Frank "Snoozer" Trushinski who played right defence for the Kitchener (Ontario) Greenshirts. According to NHL officials at the time, Trushinski lost sight in one eye playing hockey and came back and lost most of the sight in his other eye from another accident. The NHL didn't want that to happen again so it passed Bylaw 12.6.

Mrs. Trushinski once recalled her husband's problem several years after he died: "A year or so before he lost his eye, his skull was fractured in a game against the Toronto Granites hockey team. He got along seeing, but not too well.

"All his life he had a film on his left eye, so he really had trouble after the puck hit his right eye; that was during a game in 1921 when a puck hit the eye. He never saw out of it again. He was able to work a long time, though, for Schneider's, a meat company in Kitchener, Ontario."

The Trushinski Bylaw became important in March 1939 when Toronto Maple Leafs left winger George Parsons lost his left eye in an injury during an NHL game at Maple Leafs Garden against the Chicago Black Hawks.

"NHL President Frank Calder told me that I couldn't play in the NHL again," he said Parsons. "Calder said that the NHL governors wouldn't allow one-eyed players in the league because of the Trushinski precedent. Calder said the NHL didn't want that happening again."

The ruling was challenged in June 1975 when forward

Greg Neeld was drafted by the Buffalo Sabres of the NHL. Neeld had lost sight in one eye while playing amateur hockey in 1973. Neeld's lawyer Ron McMurtry threatened to sue the NHL if Neeld was kept out of the league.

The Seventh Man was a Woman
During the late 1950's teams from Twin Rivers and St. John in the Ottawa Valley League were battling for the puck when a St. John forward captured a loose puck in his defensive zone and sped free on a clean breakaway.

A little old lady, sitting in the stands, was an ardent Twin Rivers fan and was appalled at the sight of the one-on-one situation; the St. John attacker against her Twin Rivers goalie. The woman was sitting in a seat right along the sideboards which proved very convenient since the attacker skated directly in front of her as he made his way to the enemy zone.

But before he could reach the Twin Rivers blue line he was sprawled semi-conscious on the ice. The little old lady had struck him on the head with her big, black handbag. "The handle broke," noted one reporter, "and the contents spilled out onto the ice; three one-pound jars of cold cream!"

The Linesman Who Became a Body Checker
From time to time, hockey analysts discuss the qualities of superstars in terms of their instinct. "Study the great ones," said former Colorado Rockies scout Aldo Guidolin, "and you'll see that their instincts for making the right play never leave them. Even after they retire."

This was never better depicted than in the case of Ivan "Ching" Johnson, the Hall of Famer who played defence for the grand New York Rangers teams of the late 1920's and 1930's. Johnson was both notorious and revered for his thudding bodychecks which required both instinct and pinpoint timing.

Long after Johnson retired from National Hockey

League play, he retained the instinct for body contact and zest for action. He displayed this one night while acting as a linesman for an Eastern Hockey League game at Uline Arena in Washington D.C. between the New York Rovers and the Washington Lions. Play flowed back and forth with great speed when, suddenly, a Washington forward sped free on a breakaway, pushing the puck ahead of his stick.

A witness described the episode that ensued: "Johnson suddenly forgot himself. For a split second, he wasn't an official anymore; he was a Ranger defenceman all over again, and his goal was in danger. Johnson cut over in front of the fast skating Lion forward and laid him low with a bodycheck that was as hard as any you'll ever see."

A newspaperman described the Johnson check in Promethean tones. "The check was so hard," said the reporter, "it felt like it made the Lincoln Memorial shake and quiver on its granite foundation."

Having returned to his senses, Johnson resumed his chores and later went into the Washington dressing room and apologized for his faux pas. "You know," he said, "I just can't explain it. Here was that guy racing for the goal, and I just had to stop him. Why? Instinct, I guess. The old habit was too deep within me, and for a second I clean forgot where I was and what I was doing."

Shark Bait
The San Jose Sharks were not the losingest first year team in NHL history in 1991-92 but they nearly finished the season prematurely because of a non-ice-related development in mid-season.

The club was on a commercial flight to Winnipeg when the jet encountered heavy fog and had to abort one landing at the last second when the pilot missed the runway. When the plane did land, it hit the runway with a thud, causing several ceiling panels to come loose.

Defenseman Ken Hammond later observed, "I thought for a second we might be holding at 11 wins for a long time!"

A Rose Ignites a Hockey War

During the 1930's Conn Smythe and Art Ross, the respective bosses of the Toronto Maple Leafs and the Boston Bruins, grew to dislike each other more than the Hatfields and McCoys. Oneupmanship became an obsession with them and if Smythe could top Ross — or vice versa — in any way shape or form — his day was complete.

Once, Ross accused the Maple Leafs as a team and Smythe as an individual of lacking class. The next time his club visited Boston, Smythe bought ads in the Beantown dailies urging Bruin fans to come to Boston Garden "and see the team with class — the Maple Leafs."

Still not satisfied with that ploy, Smythe rented a tuxedo, replete with top hat and tails, and wore it to the game that night. Smythe had been actually aware that his archrival, Ross, was recovering from an operation for hemorrhoids. Enroute to the rink, the Toronto impresario got a brainstorm the moment he saw a vendor selling flowers.

Smythe purchased a bouquet of roses with thorns the size of cacti. On the accompanying card Smythe added a note, inscribed in Latin: "INSERT THESE UP YOUR YOU KNOW WHERE." When he reached the Maple Leafs dressing room Smythe handed the roses to his defenseman King Clancy and told Clancy to hand deliver the flowers to Ross prior to the game. As it happened Ross was sitting across the ice with some blue-blooded Bostonians when Clancy skated over with the roses.

Ross was taken aback by Smythe's seemingly gentle gesture and was further touched by the note, particularly since Ross could not read Latin. It just looked good. Ross shook Clancy's hand and then handed the roses to his aristocratic companion. The woman graciously accepted the gift until she looked at the note inviting her to shove the flowers up her derriere. Ross discovered, only too late, his companion could read Latin! As Smythe added in a postscript: "Every place Ross and I met, we fought."

A Dinner Invite Becomes a Deal
During the 1982-83 season Minnesota North Stars general manager Lou Nanne attempted to obtain forward Frank ("Seldom") Beaton from the New York Islanders in order to place Beaton on the North Stars farm club in Birmingham. Before Islanders' general manager Bill Torrey would accept the arrangement he insisted that Nanne put in writing that he would take Torrey to dinner at The Palm, a posh New York City steakhouse. Nanne agreed but certain alterations had to be made in wording to suit NHL legalese. "We had to change it officially to 'future considerations,'" Torrey admitted. "But Nanne still owes me the dinner."

Chapter Eight

Sonja Henie, Airplanes, and a Skating Bear

One of the flakier executives ever to grace the hockey scene was Tommy Lockhart, who fathered amateur hockey in the United States. Incredibly, Lockhart never put on a pair of skates. However, he was an excellent bicycle rider and runner. His hockey involvement began when Madison Square Garden president General John Reed Kilpatrick asked him to run the amateur hockey program at the Garden. From that point on, Lockhart did some bizarre things but he did get hockey going and was responsible for some of the most unusual stunts in hockey history. Here, in Lockhart's own words, are some of those stories. A couple of the best involved Sonja Henie, airplanes in the Garden, and a skating bear.

I used to have figure skaters come in and skate between periods (of hockey games). Did you know I was the one to bring Shipstad and Johnson into the Garden for the first time? They had come off the outdoor rinks in Minnesota, then played the Colony Club in Chicago. We saw their act and booked them into the Garden even though they had never skated on arena ice before. Well, that was something. There was a big difference between our Garden ice and the nightclub stuff. Maybe that's what made them.

I'll never forget their first appearance. It was between

periods of our hockey game and Shipstad and Johnson were in the dressing room, very nervous. Then they got the call to go out and they ran for the entrance, both at once. The second they hit the ice both of them fell right on their behinds the house went bananas. They got up, did their act, and came off moaning, 'Well, I guess we're finished as an act.'

A minute later one of the Garden big shots walks into their dressing room to say, 'That was a helluva act!' 'What?' they say. And he says, 'The next time you go out there, do it again.' The boys ask, "Do what?" And he says, "Fall!" That fall put the Shipstad and Johnson show on the road and led to their Ice Follies. Made a fortune for them both.

That wasn't all; we also gave Sonja Henie her debut. She had just won the Olympics and was coming to New York for a visit, so the general contacted me to say she was turning pro and that we should get her to skate at the Garden.

We had a Rover game scheduled in the afternoon and an All-Star event in the evening so we figured we'd put Sonja on in between. Some Swedish organization was in charge of selling tickets and they sold the place out, but everyone had to come to the Rover game first since they didn't know exactly when she'd go on.

What a sight. A terrific game was going on but for 30 odd minutes you could've heard a pin drop. Nobody made a sound whether the guys scored or not. Nothing. At the end of the period the teams went back to their dressing room completely disgusted. They had played fantastically but nobody reacted.

Then Sonja came out and the roof fell in. Everyone in the stands was Swedish, you see. It was some show and we decided to have Sonja skate everywhere we had an Eastern League game. Hershey, Baltimore, Atlantic City and the Rovers were the supporting cast. Still, she was a funny duck and never my cup of tea.

No doubt about it, Sonja Henie was a tough act to

follow but we managed to top her with a live bear and, believe it or not, we even flew airplanes in the Garden. Whenever somebody came in with a suggestion I'd try it. If you said you wanted to come to the hockey game and walk the length of the ice on your head Tom Lockhart would bill you. The airplanes were an example.

When I tell you we flew airplanes in the Garden I'm not kidding. It started with this big toy maker in the city. He walked into the Garden one afternoon with an idea: airplane races. He was putting out toy airplanes — the ones we had as kids that you'd run with and they'd go up in the air, their wheels turning — and he wanted us to race them on the ice. So we took a couple of players in the Metropolitan league, lined them up at one end of the rink before the Rover game, and had them skate three or four laps around the Garden and pick a winner. That's how we flew airplanes in the building.

Another guy wanted to have bicycle races on the ice. Since I was an experienced bike racer I knew it wouldn't be easy to make those turns and told the guy, "I'll prove you can't." I got on the bike and pedaled up a head of steam but when I got near the endboards I damn near plowed through them and almost killed myself. I told him if the frame could be altered it might work, but I'm glad we dropped the idea because we might have killed somebody. Working with live bears was a lot easier, believe me.

The bear was Jack Filman's idea. He was doing publicity for the Garden at the time and told me he'd seen this great act at a roller skating rink. I asked what the act was like and he replied, "There's a bear that skates." I said, "How can he skate? And if he does, he's skating on a roller floor." And Filman said, "Well, we can put him on skates, couldn't we?"

One discussion led to another and we decided that maybe we could do something with it. So we went up to take a look at the bear. The bear's owner was a foreigner and it must have taken eight hours for us to explain to him what we were trying to do and ask him to say what his bear could do. He'd tell me the bear roller skates and I'd tell him I'm not interested in roller skates, I want him to ice skate. If we'd say skates he would say he's got skates. Finally, he got the message.

We then asked how much he wanted but before he could answer I said, "I'll give you twenty dollars" and he agreed. With that settled the next trick was to get the bear into the Garden before our Sunday afternoon doubleheader. I didn't want anybody at the Garden to know there was a bear coming in because there'd be Hell to pay if they heard about it. It might start a ruckus and there'd be eighteen guys wanting to know who's going to hold the bear.

After a while I figured out the best technique. Early that Sunday morning I went down to the employees entrance on 49th Street and talked to the guy at the door. I said, "There's a cab coming here with Jack Filman and a bear."

He says, "Wha'?"

"I want you to let him in; open Room 29 and get the bear in there. And don't talk about it!"

Sure enough, Filman brings the bear, we lock him in room 29, and then he and I put our heads together because we've got a big problem — where are we going to get skates for the bear? I mean now we're dealing with a size forty shoe. We went to the Rangers equipment room and the biggest skate we could find would only go as far as the bear's instep. Meantime, Harry Westerby, the Rangers trainer, was screaming at us for taking his equipment for a bear. After we explained the act to him he suddenly got enthusiastic and finally came up with the longest skate on the hockey team.

The next question was how to put the skates on the bear. By then it was past noon and everybody in the back of the Garden was getting into the act. The Met League game was starting and people were in the building so we had to be sure the cops didn't let anybody through to the back to disturb the bear. We had decided to attach the skates to the bear's feet with rope, which we did, making it pretty secure.

All of a sudden the bear's owner chimes in that the bear can't go skating on the ice unless he goes out with him and he's got to have skates too. The search is on again; we find skates, put them on the owner, and then learn he's never been on skates in his life. He's even having trouble standing up in one place just in the room. While all this is going on the bear is using the room as a toilet and the cleanup crew had to come in with a pail and mop several times. It got so bad that the next day the Sanitation Department had to come in and disinfect the room.

Anyway, once we got a cord for the trainer to attach to the bear we were about ready. I said, "Wait a minute, we ought to tell the two teams what we're up to." It was the Rovers against the Hershey Bears. I mentioned that the bear will come out and the trainer would be with him on skates, even though he couldn't skate. We had the thing perfectly timed out and the electricians had the spotlights ready; I made the count down: "four, three, two, one!"

We bring the bear out, with the guy holding the cord. He lets five feet out, then ten feet — and falls flat on his stomach. But he wouldn't let go of that cord, he just hung on as the bear skated all over the ice pulling him around the rink.

By this time the people were up on their seats. I looked around and saw the General sitting there and enjoying it; everybody was having a great time. They were all howling but now I knew we had another problem: how were we going to get the bear off the ice? That big fella was just skating all over the place with no intentions of leaving and we had a hockey game to play. Already I had all kinds of advisors since the whole back of the Garden crowd was in on this but nobody could do a thing that worked. Finally, some woman walked up to me right out of the blue and said, "You want the bear off the ice?" I replied, "Yeah, of course I want the bear off the ice."

Next thing I know she walks out on the ice, no skates, no nothin', puts her two fingers into her mouth, whistles, and sure enough the bear comes over, pulling the Italian guy behind him like a car pulling a trailer. We took the bear back to his dressing room and along comes the General who said he thought we had a helluva act. It was so good we took it down to Hershey and it was a hit there, too.

Chapter Nine

FROM THE MOUTHS
OF FLAKES

Gordie Howe's Favorite Rocket Richard Story
Just about everyone who ever associated with The Rocket
realized that he was as intense as any player who ever put
on a pair of skates and also the most loyal.

This story may be stretching it a little but it sure makes
the point.

Rocket had retired and on this night was asked to pick
the game's three stars in Montreal.

"First," he said, "I go with my brother, Henri, because
he's such a hard worker and a good skater. Second star, I
give to Jean Beliveau because he was stickhandling so well
and played a smooth game. Third star goes to Doug Harvey
since he's such a terrific defenseman."

The broadcaster reminded Richard that he had picked
all three on the same club. He suggested that maybe somebody on the Red Wings deserved some recognition.

"Oh, yes," said The Rocket, "I'll give the fourth star to
Gordie Howe. If he hadn't scored all four goals, we would
have won!"

Gordie Howe Remembers a Doug Barkley Injury
It's no secret that hockey players wear a lot of protective
equipment but, every so often, the equipment fails. I saw
that firsthand one night when my defenseman, Doug
Barkley, took a terrific shot in the you-know-where and
went down grimacing in pain.

There's not much you can do in a situation like that except let the pain subside — whenever that ever happens — and, perhaps, cheer up your teammate, so I did my best to assure him that he hadn't lost his testicles.

I skated over to Barkley, leaned down over his head and whispered,"Doug, open your mouth for a minute."

He didn't know what the heck that was all about but, sure enough, he opened his mouth.

With that, I leaned back over him and said, "THERE THEY ARE!"

Dave Taylor's Favorite Characters
I played against Tiger Williams when he was with Vancouver and had him for a teammate in Los Angeles. He was a real piece of work, especially his mouth. On or off the ice, he never stopped talking, always insulting the opposition. God forbid he ever learned your ethnic background, then he'd REALLY give it to you.

Tiger was a win-at-all-costs type guy but away from the rink, a devoted family man who had a love for the outdoors. His temper was such on the ice that you never knew what to expect from him.

I recall him once getting a penalty, skating to the penalty box and then, when he got there, he started throwing chairs out onto the ice. Another time he slammed the door and all the glass fell out.

When he was with the Canucks they came to L.A. one night and he really got out of hand. The referee finally threw him out of the game. As Williams was leaving the ice, a fan threw a beer on his head.

In a split-second Tiger went right up into the stands after the guy. Later on some reporters asked why he went after the fan. With a straight face, Williams said,"I just wanted to visit an old friend."

I remember him also being ejected while playing for the Kings. He went straight to the dressing room and destroyed a TV set.

Peter Stemkowski was another character I liked but for different reasons than Tiger although Peter was quick with the words as well. Before coming to L.A., Stemmer had been with the Rangers and even did some radio work on a local New York station.

He'd never let us forget it either. At day-of-game skates, Peter would stand up in the middle of the dressing room and give morning traffic and weather reports.

We had a team rule that everyone had to be on the ice for practice. Stemmer would arrive at the rink wearing a full dress suit, go into the dressing room, take off his shoes and put on a pair of skates. Then, he'd walk onto the ice in his suit and skate for a minute or two and step right off. He figured he had done what the coaches had wanted him to do; namely be on the ice — regardless of how long or in what condition.

The coaches just shook their heads and laughed. They all knew that it was Stemmer's last year in the league and there was nothing they could do.

Goalies are always different but Gary Simmons was *really* different. He had tattoos all over his body.

During my rookie year with the Kings our number one goalie was Rogie Vachon, who was at the top of his game. Simmons was the backup and hardly ever played. In one stretch Rogie played about 20 straight games until they finally put Gary in for a game. He won it, 3-2, and after the game reporters interviewing him asked when his next start would be. His reply: "WHAT DO YOU THINK I AM, A MACHINE!"

Gary didn't think of himself as a goalie but rather as a cowboy. He would ride around on a motorcycle in cowboy boots, a T-shirt and jeans. During training camp, we were supposed to do an exercise that consisted of running up 90th Street outside The Forum to a little mountain in a park where we would stretch and do calisthenics.

It was only a half-mile jog but Gary would ride up the hill on his motorcycle in his cowboy hat, T-shirt and jeans and pass by all of us. And he got away with it!

Then there was Dean Kennedy, who played defense for us for a while. He used a personal trainer who would put him in an almost hypnotic state. Then Kennedy would take hockey sticks and break them across a punching bag. It was a type of mind conditioning.

Every team has loners but we had an unusual one named Don Kozak who always spent a lot of time by himself. The strange thing was that he had a big following among the fans who called him Krazy Kozy for his reckless way on the ice. Even though he wasn't a big guy he'd throw his weight around.

Kozy never wore a helmet and he was quite a sight with his long hair flowing as he flew around the rink. The fans loved him and some of his group would come to games wearing hats with a revolving red light on top.

Charlie Hodge Remembers Doug Harvey

Before Doug made it up to the Montreal Canadiens, he played senior hockey in the old Quebec Senior League with the Montreal Royals. Doug liked to party in those days, which would be the mid-1940s, and sometimes he'd be up til the wee, small hours of the morning.

On this particular occasion, Doug had left the party and was looking high and low for a taxicab but couldn't find one. There was nothing around but a milkman who was delivering his bottles with an old horse and cart.

When Harvey noticed that the milkman was carrying his bunch of bottles to a house, Doug climbed into the wagon, grabbed the reins and drove the horse and wagon right to his home. That poor milkman must still be wondering why his horse ever took off on him.

Kevin Lowe Visits Hugh Hefner's Playboy Mansion with Gretz and Mess.

An invitation to three bachelors to Hugh Hefner's Playboy Mansion is not something that comes to NHL players every day. So, when Mark Messier, Wayne Gretzky and I got the invite our juices were flowing.

Too bad we didn't get our transportation arrangements straight. The word given to us was that we should hire a limousine and get out at a big rock at the mansion gate. The rock supposedly was a security checkpoint, complete with a camera which delivered pictures to the mansion. It also had a speaker system enabling you to talk to the rock. They told us that once we got to the rock, we should have the driver take us in.

Wayne decided that it would take too long to get a limo, so we opted for a taxicab and told the driver to take us to the Playboy Mansion. But when we got to the outside gates, we felt a little silly taking a taxi inside when the others arrived in a stretch limo. We paid off the cabby and decided to walk the rest of the way, right up the secret rock.

When we told the rock who we were, an attendant opened the gate and said, "Just have your driver bring you up."

Our driver was gone by now but we weren't upset. We figured the mansion was just around the corner, so we started walking up the hill. We walked and walked — and walked. The more we walked, the more cameras we could hear zeroing in on us from the trees. All the while, Mark kept saying, "If Hefner walks by, I'm gonna slug the son-of-a-gun in his pyjamas and pipe."

Meanwhile, we're STILL walking. After what seemed to be hours, we arrived at the mansion. One of Hefner's public relations people came out and announced, "You guys should feel honored to be here, because Mister Hefner rarely does this — but because of Mister Gretzky, he's making an exception."

All of a sudden, our night got brighter. A dozen beautiful girls appeared, so we did what was natural and mingled with them before sitting down to dinner.

Right on cue, Hefner himself marched in, wearing pyjamas and smoking his pipe. He dropped over to chat with us. Fortunately, Mark never did deliver that sucker punch.

Kevin Lowe's Favorite Colin Campbell Stories
When I broke in with the Oilers in Edmonton's first NHL season, 1979-80, we had quite a bunch of characters but the prize of them all, when it came to jokers, was Colin Campbell.

A husky, little defenseman, Campbell had a whimsical sense of humor and he wasn't above pulling pranks on our exalted leader, Glen Sather, who then was coach and general manager of the team.

A Campbell specialty was the Leaky Coffee Container Routine. He'd puncture the bottom of a styro foam coffee container with a tiny needle. The hole would be big enough for liquid to seep through but small enough to be invisible to the naked eye.

Colin preferred singling out Sather as a victim because Slats was such a classy dresser. His suits were impeccably tailored and very expensive, I might add.

Once Sather began drinking, the coffee would make its way down his chin. Of course, he soon realized he had been had but then he'd try to pretend that nothing was happening.

Another of Colin's routines I labelled the Why Don't You Get Out Of The Toilet routine. That one he'd pull off in the locker room after a workout. He'd start by taking a pair of pants, attach them to socks and then insert the socks into a pair of shoes. He'd arrange it so that someone from the outside would think one of the guys was sitting on the can.

Sooner or later the guys would be pounding on the door, trying to get into the john themselves. Since there were so many rookies on the team at the time, we weren't wise to Campbell's tricks and he had quite a few victims to play around with for a while.

Al Secord's Favorite Hangover Story
When I was with the Bruins one of my Boston teammates was Dwight Foster. The night before a road trip he had too much rum and had to be up for a six a.m. flight. As soon as

he got into his plane seat, Foster just passed out and I mean *passed out!*

He was leaning against the window with his mouth wide open which was a perfect set up for a few tricks.

I put three inches worth of shaving cream on his glasses with a couple of raisins on top. He was so out of it, he didn't even respond when we put little pieces of newspaper on his lips. Every time Dwight exhaled, the stuff would go flying. And it was even funnier when he woke up and realized what we had done.

Stan Smyl on Colin Campbell's Come-uppance

One of the most satisfying things for a player is getting even with one of the club's practical jokers. I had the pleasure of that experience when I was playing for Vancouver in 1981-82, the year the Canucks went to the Stanley Cup finals.

By far the worst prankster on the team was Colin ("Soupy") Campbell who managed to get everybody at one time or another.

Well, we finally got beat out in the finals in four straight to the Islanders and were ready to pack it in for the season. There was just one more thing; we had to pose for the team picture.

Everybody, by this time, had become fed up with Soupy's jokes and the general feeling was that we had to get even with him somehow.

Someone found out that Campbell had just bought a new car and drove it to the arena the afternoon of the picture-taking.

While we were getting ready for the photo, somebody stole his car keys and got a hold of the car.

Campbell and the rest of us were on the ice having our pictures taken when, without warning, a guy drove Soupy's brand new car on to the ice.

It was covered from top to bottom with shaving cream.

That quieted down Campbell until the following year.

The Daffy World of Tom McVie

(If anyone qualifies as a Flake of Winter, it is Tom McVie. Although he never made it to the NHL as a player, McVie spent a lifetime playing minor pro hockey and another lifetime coaching on all levels, right up to the bigs.

The 1991-92 season marked McVie's first full year in the NHL, after several seasons in the AHL with Maine and Utica. Ironically, McVie was replaced by Herb Brooks after the 1992 playoffs. Nonetheless, the gravel-voiced, rubber-faced leader is proud of a record that includes stints with two of the worst teams in NHL history, the Washington Capitals and the Winnipeg Jets. He's now assistant coach of the Boston Bruins.

"Somebody once told me," chuckles McVie, "that if you really want to be a good coach, get some good players. Now that's what I call good advice."

During a spate of interviews at the Byrne Meadowlands Arena in New Jersey and the Devils' practice rink in nearby West Orange, McVie spun several tales out of his playing and coaching past.)

When I played in the Western League the NHL only had six teams so the minors were stocked with plenty of guys who were on a major league level only there wasn't any room for them. We also had our share of characters and one of them was a real tough — and I mean TOUGH — defenseman named Connie Madigan.

Because he was so mean I gave him the nickname Mad Dog but Connie was very finicky about it. He'd let me use the nickname but no one else was allowed to use it otherwise he'd have a fit.

Naturally, the name got around —which didn't make Madigan very happy — and one night we're coming out on the ice for a road game and the fans noticed him and started barking. Well, that's all Connie needed to hear; he was really going.

So, anyway the game started and soon after he ran someone on the opposition. The referee whistles Madigan off for a penalty and the hometown announcer figured he'd get the crowd going so he broadcasts, "TWO MINUTES FOR CHARGING ON MAD DOG MADIGAN."With that, the crowd started barking big time.

Connie was so angry that the public address announcer called him Mad Dog that he skated over to the penalty timekeeper's bench — where the PA guy also sits — to hit the guy with the microphone.

Well, there were three of them sitting there and when the announcer with the mike sees Mad Dog skating over he, quick-like, passes the mike to the next guy and the three of them were moving the microphone back and forth as if it was a hot potato. Finally, Madigan swung and they put one of the guys on a stretcher.

Not that I was an angel, far from it. I'll give you an example: when I played for Portland in the old Western League, one of our stops was Los Angeles. We'd check into a hotel and then the day of a game we'd have a team meeting down by the pool.

Our coach was a former NHL defenseman named Hal Laycoe and he was a stickler for punctuality; we were never allowed to be late.

On this particular day, Laycoe called a meeting for Noon down by the pool and all the guys were there in plenty of time, sitting around waiting for the coach to begin. Except, I wasn't there yet.

It was one minute to twelve and still no McVie, so everybody's wondering what happened to me and what Laycoe will do. Meantime, I was in my room, three stories above the pool and I should tell you that I had been a three-meter diving champion when I was a young guy. I had done a lot of diving off bridges and stuff like that.

Anyway, with the final seconds ticking off before Noon, I walked out to the balcony, climbed to the edge and dove right off from the third story into the pool.

The splash almost drowned everybody. Down to the bottom of the pool I went and when I came up it was about ten seconds before Noon. "Coach," I shouted, "you can't fine me for being late!"

I may have seemed like a clown at times but deep down I always took my hockey seriously both as a player and a coach. My wife once told me that I had a mistress. I said, "Who would that be?" And she'd say, "Hockey is your mistress."

She always knew that hockey is first and she's second. We've got a great family, three great sons but hockey has always been more important to me than anything. People get mad at me for saying it but that's too bad because that's the way it is.

I say that because I've done everything in hockey, even

driving the bus. When I stopped playing, they told me that I'd have to start in the lowest league if I wanted to become a coach. I went to the old Eastern League at the age of 37 and the only way I could get the job was to be a player-coach.

Travelling in that league was unbelievable. We had teams up in the Northeast but one down in Jacksonville, Florida. We'd get on a bus and go straight down. A lot of the time our driver would be just short of falling asleep behind the wheel so I'd trade places with him and I'd drive the bus as well. I played, I coached and drove the team bus.

The only thing I didn't do was referee but I can tell you I had plenty of run-ins with the officials. Once when I was still playing we had a big game in Los Angeles and a fellow named Lloyd Gilmour was refereeing.

On this particular play one of our guys shot the puck and, somehow, it found an opening UNDER the net but it didn't go in the legal way. At least that's the way Gilmour called it; he said it wasn't a goal and emphatically waved it off.

Our coach, Laycoe, was fit to be tied and wasn't about to let Gilmour off the hook. Instead of sending five guys out for the next face-off, Laycoe did everything he could to embarrass the official and delay the game. Laycoe said, "We're not starting the game until they count that goal!

Laycoe then sent me on one of many missions across the ice to the referee. I'd dash up to Gilmour, stop short and throw a ton of ice shavings all over him. Then, I'd convey the coach's message.

Gilmour shot back, "You tell Laycoe that *I'm* running the game, not him."

With that, I took off for Laycoe, skated like a madman across the ice and shouted all over our bench to give Laycoe the reply.

By this time the crowd is dying laughing. Now Laycoe actually stepped on the ice and Gilmour came chasing me across the rink and threw the coach right out of the game. Then, he turned to me and said, "You're going right into the penalty box!"

Hearing that, I skated as fast as I could and dove head-first right over the boards into the box.

The crowd was just dying laughing but Gilmour wasn't amused. He threw me right out of the game.

Another fellow who wasn't amused was an L.A. defenseman by the name of Red Bonush. He was a big, tough guy who couldn't see too good. These were the days before soft contact lenses had been invented so Red would play without glasses and squint a lot.

On this particular night, we were playing against his club and he was coming around his own net and I yelled out to him, "Red! Red!"

He obviously couldn't tell who it was, friend or foe, but he passed the puck right on my stick and I smacked it right in their net.

Well, it was bad enough I coaxed him into making the bad pass and then I scored on it, but then I skated up to him and patted Red on the back and said, "Thanks for the pass."

The next thing I knew I woke up in the dressing room. Red took off his glove and drove me right in the head and knocked me cold. I really had it coming and he just about killed me.

From that point on, whenever we played against his club, Red would chase me around the rink and I'd play good just out of fear.

I'd also have a helluva lot of fun and I'd get laughs from my teammates. One of my favorite routines was stuffing a puck in my mouth because my mouth IS big enough to handle a puck. I played with a fellow named Charlie Holmes and what I would do is I'd stuff a puck in my mouth and then we'd scrimmage and when the puck went over the boards, I'd say, "Well, Charlie, I got one right here!" And I'd spit out a puck.

That story got exaggerated. It started out with one puck, then two and now they've got it all the way up to four. But it really was only one although I had a lot of variations on the trick. When I was in Dayton, I'd go on the ice and someone would skate in on me and shoot the puck.

I'd try to block it and then someone would pat me on the back and the puck would come out of my mouth. The other guys would howl at that stuff.

A lot of the stuff I picked up from other coaches and a lot of it I discarded right away. One of the weirdest coaches of all was a guy named Bill Fraser, who had been a goaltender and was nicknamed Legs because he was so tall. Fraser was one of the first really mean goalies. He had this habit of swinging his stick over the net to clip forwards as they went behind him.

He was pretty mean as a coach, too. One of his gimmicks was "The Door Trick," which was a way of hurting the opposition. In our rink, for a time, the door to the bench opened out on to the ice instead of in the way they do in all the rinks. What Fraser would do is keep an eye on our opposition and when there was somebody on the other team who was back checking and he didn't like, Legs would open the damn door, let the guy run into it and try to kill the guy.

Legs may have been THE person who forced a rule that all doors had to open into the bench not out to the ice.

When I played for him, he'd be smoking cigars all the time and he didn't give a damn whether you liked it or not. I have one memory of him when we were having a team meal. He came in and threw a cigar right in my soup bowl. What was I going to say to him? He'd goddamn kill me if I did say anything.

Other times, I'd be sitting in the hotel lobby, reading the sports section and Fraser would sneak up, light a match and I'd wind up holding a burning newspaper.

When I started coaching I had a completely mistaken approach to handling players. My coaches I had played for were miserable SOBs and I assumed that that was the approach I was supposed to take. For the first three years behind the bench I was a miserable son-of-a-bitch. It was all because of the memories I had of people like Fraser.

I can remember walking down a hotel hallway and I would see the player up ahead and when I got to that spot, he was gone. He'd just disappear. And when you did walk by the guy, he wouldn't even look at you, wouldn't say, "Good morning." That's the way it was. I would turn and walk away rather than encounter a player.

After the third year, I changed and it's an interesting story how it came about. A player I had skated with for years knew me as an off-the-wall guy but now he saw I was different. We went for lunch one day and he said, "What's the matter with you? You're the most miserable son-of-a-bitch I've ever seen." When he asked me why, I said, "Because I'm the coach. That's why! You have to be that way when you're the coach." He couldn't believe it. "Tommy," he said, "that's not you. Keep it up and you're not going to last long." From that point on, little by little, my true personality came out.

Of course that didn't mean I got the results I wanted. After coaching for three years, I thought I could make all my guys play that tough, driving, forechecking game because when the Islanders won four Stanley Cups, they won that way. I worked on trying to get my guys to play that way but after three years I said I must be doing something wrong because I couldn't get my guys to finish their checks. So, one year I'm at the draft and I met Freddie Shero and I asked him how I could get every one of them to finish their checks.

He said, "C'mon, Tommy, that's simple." I said, "Simple! I've been trying for years. How do you do it'" He said, "It's easy. You take the ten guys who do it and eliminate the eight who won't. Then, get a new bunch of eight — and then everyone will finish their checks." What he was getting at is that no matter what you'd do with the original eight, no matter how hard you teach, they come out of the crib not being able to finish checks. They either do it or they don't. And size has nothing to do with it.

In my business you're not in a comfort zone, you walk the tightrope. Coaches don't get paid for coaching, they get paid for winning. Me, I've been fired more times than Clint Eastwood's Magnum. When I worked for the Flyers in

Maine, they sold the whole franchise just to get rid of me. No wonder they call me "The Rodney Dangerfield of Hockey." Once, I was called up from the farm team in Maine to coach the New Jersey Devils for the rest of the 1983-84 season. That Summer I told (Devils' owner) John McMullen his team didn't have any talent. I said it was so bad that if I stayed, it wouldn't be long before he'd have to fire me. I said I'd rather develop young players for the organization in the AHL. Mr. Mac just looked at me and said, "You mean you'd rather go back to Maine, earn half as much money and ride the buses for 20,000 miles?" When I said, "Yes," he just shook his head and said, "Tommy, you may be a good hockey man but you're not very smart."

My first NHL job was in Washington and we had a BAD team. Once we were beaten badly by the Kings in Los Angeles. We didn't have assistant coaches in those days and I was going up the ramp at the Forum, all alone, after the game. I looked down at the street and I could see the players laughing and jostling while they're piling into cabs for a night in L.A. and I'm not sure a tear didn't roll down my cheek. But I get to my hotel near the race track and on one side of the wall is a huge window. I'm standing there, looking out and the thought actually occurs to me that I should go back to the wall, take a run and dive right through the window.

It's so scary that I said to myself, "Hey, man, you ought to get out of here." So, I go down to the lobby and I see our equipment man, Keith Parker. I tell him how I was thinking about jumping and he looks at me and said, "The way you're going, you'd have landed in the swimming pool and ruined your new suit!"

I once got so mad at my team I said it wouldn't matter if the bridge collapsed with the team bus on it because my players "floated" so much, they'd never drown.

A few years later, when I was coaching the lousy Devils team, we were in Vancouver. This was after another lopsided loss. A reporter asked me, "Are you the same Tom McVie who coached the Washington Capitals to 150 losses in three years,the same Tom McVie who coached the Winnipeg Jets to 106 losses in two years, 30 in a row in 1979-80?"

After I told him that I was, he said, "And now you have THIS awful team. Do you ever think of doing something else for a living?"

I faked a shocked expression and replied, "Me, give up coaching? Hell, no, it's the only thing I know how to do well!"

I knew I was a good coach but the only one else who did was my wife — and she's not a general manager. Of course, my wife has been the target of some of my humor; like when I was hired as coach in Portland, Maine. I opened my acceptance speech by thanking my wife "who's stood beside me all these years." Then, I proceeded to list in detail the spots I had been as coach, place by place. Finally, a look of realization crossed my face and I said, "Now that I think about it, *the woman has been nothing more than a jinx*" I once told my wife that I didn't love her as much as I loved hockey — but I loved her more than baseball.

Now I can afford to joke about it because I'm the only guy walking the planet to have coached three expansion teams and lived to talk about them. And having been around so long, I can make jokes about the kids that come up. For example, in 1991-92, the Devils promoted a young goalie from the St.Hyacinth Juniors, Martin Brodeur. Somebody told me that he was born in 1972. I said, "I have messages on my desk older than that."

The low point in my career had to be Washington. It was my first NHL job and I gave my soul. I put the team ahead of my family and health. I took a day off once with my wife and when I came back Danny Belisle was in my coach's chair. They said, "You're gone!" Now I take my chair with me and never go on vacations. You have to remember I was a guy going to the rink and spending 16 hours a day there. After I got fired I had16 hours a day with nothing to do but stand on the front porch like an idiot waving at cars.

Losing is no fun, even if you have a terrible team. I remember taking over that bad Washington team on December 30, 1975 and we were 3-28-5. I'd coach 12 games before we won one but I'd always be gung-ho for the next workout. "Gentlemen," I would say, "I have these things planned for today. We'll do some two-on-ones, some three-on-ones..." And I saw the looks on them, like "This guy is bleepin' crazy." I went on and on with it and they just leaned on their sticks and listened. Finally, I asked if anybody had anything to say.

One of my defensemen, Bob Paradise, said, "Why are we doing this when we know we're going to bleeping lose anyway?" I looked at him and said, "Well, then, why don't we all go to (Owner) Abe Pollin's office and tell him we are disbanding the team?"

When John Ferguson was my boss in Winnipeg, he thought I was pretty flaky one day after I benched the great Bobby Hull. Fergie asked why and I told him he showed up late and that's why he couldn't play.

Fergie thought I was joking. Then he went out, kicked the door and came back in. "Let me ask you a question; do you know it's Tuxedo Night and that we've got a full house and Hockey Night In Canada and Sports Illustrated are here?" I said, sorry, rules are rules.

So, Fergie went out again and came back and said, "Let me ask you one more thing; do you know Bobby Hull is one of the owners of this team?" I said I sort of heard something about it. But I still wouldn't budge.

You have to remember that Fergie and I had grown up together in a tough section of Vancouver. Totally exasperated by me, Fergie finally throws up his hand and says, "Growing up, I knew you had guts, but I didn't realize they were that big."

P.S. Without Bobby Hull, we went out and won the game.

More than ten years later, people ask me if I've changed as a coach and I tell them I'm still the same abrasive, hard-driving screamer I always was. All that changed is that when I came to Jersey the second time, I had better players. Like always, good players make smart coaches.

You can only push it hard for so long before you blow a tire or throw a rod. And no matter how well you drive, sooner or later Mario Andretti is going to blow on by you because he's got more horses under his hood than you do.

The second time around in Jersey I had more horses under my hood than I did the first time. But I also had a melting pot of French-Canadians, Russians, Swedes, a guy who was born in Haiti (Claude Vilgrain), Americans, a Finn and, of course, Canadians. When I got this melting pot, I decided to do the very best because these were the cards I was dealt, but it wasn't always easy.

One day I told Claude Lemieux, one of my best scorers, what it was like to coach the team. "Claudie," I said, "I got four guys who don't understand a word I say. I've got ten who understand but don't want to do what I tell 'em. And I've got another four who understand but can't do what I tell 'em."

No complaints, though. When it comes to hockey, it's almost like I'm Karnac the Magnificent. It's scary some of the things I say about certain players. I see the way these guys act and I'll say something to somebody and say what's going to happen and a month later it happens. Others will say, "Tommy, how the hell did you know that?" I know, I just know.

Bill Chadwick is Left Holding the Bag

(A member of the Hockey Hall of Fame, Bill Chadwick was headed for a starry stickhandling career when a freak injury deprived him of sight in one eye. Despite the setback, Chadwick began refereeing and worked his way right up to the NHL where he became one of the game's best officials.

One of the toughest rinks in which Chadwick refereed was Chicago Stadium and the 1944 playoff between the Blackhawks and Canadiens was one that Chadwick never will forget.)

The Canadiens had won the opener, 5-1, in Montreal and now the series moved to Chicago. I was working the game with the linesmen Jim Primeau and Ed Mepham.

It was 2-1 for Montreal in the third period with the Canadiens Punch Line — Rocket Richard, Elmer Lach and Toe Blake — on the attack. Chicago had a defenseman named George Allen who was on the ice trying to break up the rush but Lach managed to tie up Allen in front of the Blackhawks net.

"Hold! Hey, Chadwick, he's holding me." Allen was so excited that he broke away from Lach and chased over to me, shouting for a penalty. I still hadn't blown the whistle but Allen was arguing as if play had stopped.

Allen kept on beefing and, meanwhile, Lach was now unchecked in front of the Blackhawks goal. Elmer chased after the puck and relayed it to The Rocket. He easily scored and the Canadiens were now leading 3-1.

Allen was fit to be tied and so were the 18,000 fans jamming Chicago Stadium. "No, no, no!" Allen was chirping at me and I shouted back, "Yes, yes, yes." The goal counted but the crowd picked up on Allen's complaint and began tossing every kind of object on the ice.

You wouldn't believe the objects that came flying down from above; cigarette lighters, keys, nuts, bolts and a pair of false teeth.

A guy could get hurt out there so I moved to what I thought was the safest place on the ice, dead center. It was no fun, even as the crowd switched to tossing galoshes, rubbers, boots and even chairs. Finally, I called over my linesman.

"Jim," I said, "the president (Red Dutton) is sitting over there in a box seat. Go ask him what I should do."

Primeau skated over to the president's box and passed on my message. Dutton leaned over and listened intently as if he was going to deliver some sage advice. I was hoping that Dutton would bail me out.

At last, Primeau skated back to me at center ice.

"What did he say?" I wondered.

"Dutton says," Primeau explained, "you got yourself into this. Now get yourself out of it!"

Todd Gill's Most Embarrassing Moment (as told on Don Cherry's "Grapevine")

We were on a road trip stop at Boston during the years when Harold Ballard still owned the Maple Leafs. He was well on in years and sickly at the time. Harold liked to travel with the team but he had taken sick and returned to Toronto. Just by chance, I wound up in Ballard's hotel suite.

It was unbelievable; the biggest suite I had ever seen. The first thing I decided to do once I settled in was to get something to eat. I phoned roomed service and ordered a pizza sent up to the room.

After the pizza was delivered, I decided to relax and since I had only one set of clothes I didn't want to stain the suit with any pizza sauce. I figured, what the heck, I'll take all my clothes off and enjoy the pizza nude.

I ate the pizza and once I was finished I decided to put the pizza box outside the room so the chambermaid could dispose of it. I opened the door, peeked out to make sure that nobody was around — I was still in my birthday suit — then quickly walked out and put down the box.

Before I could turn around and get back in the door to the suite slammed behind me, automatically locking.

Here I am out in the hallway in my birthday suit and with empty box of pizza. There were phones at the end of the hallway so I went to them and called the desk to see if they had a key to open the door, but the phones were dead.

What to do?

I decided to knock on some doors in the hopes of finding a teammate or someone connected with the team but got no answer.

Finally I decided to knock on ANY door and, sure enough, a man answered. When he saw me all naked his eyes were popping out of his head. What would you do if you answered a door and there was a guy with nothing but a pizza box wrapped around him?

After getting over the shock, the guy let me in and I phoned the front desk. A few minutes later they opened my door.

Just Having Fun

Buzzy Deschamps, who played both American and Eastern League hockey, and currently is in the hockey equipment business, has a favorite Jim McKenny story.

"Jimmy was a young Toronto Maple Leaf defenseman when Red Kelly was coaching the team," says Deschamps. "In those days the Islanders had their four-straight Stanley Cup dynasty and visitors almost never won at Nassau Coliseum.

"On this day the Leafs came to the Island having lost four in a row and were in a pretty deep funk. Kelly, who was a very low-key individual, called a pre-game meeting. Just about all the guys were very serious about it and Red added to the atmosphere when he started talking.

"Red talked a bit about the Islanders and then he wound up by saying, 'If you guys get your act together and win tonight, you can really start having some fun.'

"McKenny is sitting there with a straight face but when Red finishes, Jimmy pops up and says, 'If I was having any more fun, Red, I couldn't stand it.'"

Buy a Number

Hall of Famer Denis Potvin's number five was retired by the New York Islanders but Potvin reveals that he always had hoped to wear number seven rather than five.

"When I joined the team in 1973," Potvin recalls, "I asked for seven because that's the number I always wore in Junior hockey. I asked the trainer and he said, 'Maybe we can do it.' The next thing I know there's a note on my locker that said: 'If you want that number, pay me $500.' It was signed by Germaine Gagnon, a forward on the club. I stayed with number five !"

Bryan ("Bugsy") Watson on the First Game After a Trade
I had been dealt from the Montreal Canadiens to the Detroit Red Wings, and in my next game, I wound up skating against my old teammates. Believe it or not, on my very first shift on the ice, the Canadiens scored *three goals.*

After the first period, we returned to the dressing room, and I got up looked around and said, "Hey, guys, is there something wrong with the deal? Don't you like it?"

Michael Barnett Recalls Ace Bailey's Christmas Caper
When Wayne Gretzky was breaking in with the Edmonton Oilers, Bill("Cowboy") Flett and Garnet ("Ace") Bailey were winding down their careers.During the early part of the season Ace would leave his wife, Cathy, in the Boston area and bring her out to Edmonton in time for Christmas.

Before she came, Ace rented an apartment but he thought it would be nice if he got a house for Cathy before she got to Edmonton. Sure enough, Ace found a house he liked and made arrangements to rent it, but he never got inside the place.

At least not yet. Cathy hadn't arrived but it was already the start of the Christmas season and some parties were going on and one of them involved some of the Oilers, including Ace, Wayne and Cowboy.

After the boys left the party, they decided to once and for all check out Bailey's new rented house. So, Ace led them to the place. It was the dead of night with not much light around. Bailey finally found the key and tried to open the door but he couldn't seem to make it work.

He figured he had a bum key or that there was something wrong with the lock. But Cowboy was determined to get Ace into his new digs, so he walked around to the back of the house and started playing around with the garage door. All of a sudden, it sprang open with a clatter and a bang. Unbeknownst to Cowboy, an elderly couple were in bed inside the house.

When they heard the noise at the garage door, the old guy crawled on his hands and knees to the telephone and quietly called the police telling them his house was in the process of being robbed.

Meanwhile, Cowboy had climbed up the back of the house and was busy trying to jimmy open one of the rear windows when there's a siren, a police car and a search-light beaming right into Flett's face.

The cop immediately recognized him and said, "Cow-boy, what the devil are you doing here?"

Flett explained that they were trying to get into Bailey's new house.

The cop laughed. "Don't you know that you're climbing up the wrong house. Ace's place is two doors down!"

Well, Bailey was so happy to get into his house that he forgot that Christmas was just around the corner and so was Cathy. When she arrived, Cathy looked around the house and exclaimed, "Ace, it sure would be nice if we had a Christmas tree for Christmas."

"Think nothing of it, my dear," Bailey promised. "I will take care of that little thing immediately."

Ace departed and Cathy began putting things in order. But before she could turn around, there was her husband standing in the living room with a beautiful tree, ready for decorating.

She praised Ace for making such a dandy choice and then walked into the kitchen to finish cleaning the dishes. While she was at it, Cathy looked out of the kitchen win-dow to the backyard.

There, staring her in the face was the freshly cut stump of a tree.

Ace was duly admonished and as soon as the Christ-mas holiday was over, he took the tree into the backyard and tried to nail it to the stump!

Bob Froese Gets Bad Advice on Guy Lafleur

After I became one of the Rangers' goalies, Chris Nilan was traded from Montreal to New York. The first thing I did was get the "book" on the Canadiens' players because we were about to play them. Nilan was the obvious choice for me to get a scouting report.

Chris told me that The Flower had a cannon shot and that I should watch out for it. That was fair enough. I had known enough about Lafleur so all I figured I had to do was be vigilant and watch for his blast.

So, now the game is on and in a very short time, Lafleur broke down the wing. I was ready on my tip-toes and said, "There's no way I'm gonna get beat by this guy."

I'm all keyed up and Guy winds up and just about fans on the shot. He gets off a weak slapper — soft and low to the ice — and went right between my legs. So much for scouting reports.

While the crowd was roaring, Nilan skated over to me and winked, "I guess he changed his style a little bit."

Al Iafrate and the Brophy Diet Plan

This was in my rookie year with the Maple Leafs; I was really overweight; maybe about 255 pounds. I knew I had to drop a lot of pounds and in a week I was down to 240, but still in horrible shape.

We had an exhibition game — John Brophy was our assistant coach — and I was dogging it and getting abused all over the ice. I was getting real tired and it's only my second shift and I'm stumbling around like an idiot.

I go to get off the ice and Brophy, who was on the bench, jumped to the front and screamed at me to keep my fat ass on the ice.

Now I'm exhausted, so I skate to the other end of the bench and am about to walk through the door opening when Brophy runs over and slams the door shut. This time, he screamed, "Stay out there, you fat piece of shit!"

What could I do? I stayed out another half a minute and finally Brophy allowed me to get on the bench.

Derek Sanderson Remembers...

(When Derek Sanderson broke in with the Big, Bad Bruins of the late 1960's, he quickly emerged as one of hockey's most colorful characters. He also became a splendid storyteller — and still is as a member of the Bruins broadcast team. Here he tells a tale about a pro hockey ritual known as The Shave. ,)

The Shave is a ritual that has been part of hockey for a long time and I, unfortunately, was a victim. It happened to me as a rookie and was a pretty horrid affair.

What happens is that the victim is brought into a room — usually by some subterfuge — stripped from head to toe and then placed in a horizontal position. When I was a Bruin, our goalie Eddie Johnston was the official shaver because he was the oldest player on the team.

His job was to shave every piece of hair off the rookie, without benefit of shaving cream or water. That meant he shaved the chest hairs and the underarm hairs. In fact, ALL hair.

I thought I'd get nailed in training camp but, somehow, I escaped and nothing happened to me in October, November or December, for that matter, right up to New Year's Eve 1967.

We were in Detroit on December 31, 1967 and it was four in the morning. I was fast asleep in my hotel room when the phone rang. It was Bobby Orr. "Derek, come up to the room — I've got two girls who want to meet you." Sounded good. So I got dressed, eager as hell, zipped upstairs and walked into his room.

There were nine guys, including Eddie Johnston. I looked a little more closely and noticed that Eddie had the razor in his hand. They got me good, stripped me all the way down and then spread-eagled me on the floor. Eddie went straight for my calves and started shaving them completely. It hurt like hell.

It's never a very neat job. They lacerate you some and then, while you're bleeding, they throw shaving lotion on the wounds. It really is no fun.

I finally got up and could hardly maneuver. I was stiff and couldn't walk straight for a couple of days. Believe me, that's a tough thing to explain to a girl. They usually didn't believe it anyway. Like, who's crazy enough to shave a man's hair up and down his body?

Obviously, hockey players were!

Sanderson Imitates Coach Harry Sinden

We were always told to respect the coach and we did, when he was directly in front of us. But when Harry Sinden wasn't around, he became the butt of humor.

One day I decided to imitate Sinden. Everybody on the club knew the way he acted, how he looked. So I put my hands in my pockets the way Harry did at the start of a pep talk, dropped my head the way Harry did and then took a couple of deep breaths, which were typical.

I took a quick turn on my heels, looked at one of the players and then stared at the floor. "C'mon now, guys," I said. "We blew that one last night. We gotta be going. Now, for God's sake, get going! Get in the corners. Throw it in and go and get it. Chase 'em in there. Make sure. Rush 'em. Make sure they make the bad play. Make sure they can't get any time to get to do anything they want to do. C'mon now, guys, let's get on the right track."

I was breaking up the players but, unknown to me, Harry had walked into the dressing room right in the middle of my impersonation. I just kept going with my act. Meanwhile, all the guys were watching Harry standing by the door, and the guys were dying by this time. Laughter is like good food, so I just kept on going. Finally, Eddie Johnston got worried, leaned over and said,"Turk, look behind you, for heaven's sakes, before you get too carried away."

I turned around and there was Harry.

"Keep going," Harry insisted, "you're doing a great job. But you'd better not lose this game tonight or you'll be in deep trouble." Before he left, I went over and said, "Sorry about that, Harry." But he just laughed it off.

Turk Breaks a Cardinal Rule

In baseball they say you should never mention that a pitcher has a no-hitter late in a game for fear that it would spoil his good luck. It's the same thing in hockey with a goalie's shutout late in a game.

On the Bruins, we once had a young goalie named Joe Junkin, who was used when our regular goalies, Eddie Johnston and Gerry Cheevers, were unavailable.

Junkin didn't play all that much but on this particular night he was super. He was so good that he had himself a shutout with only a few minutes left in the game.

When the clock showed four minutes, Joe skated to the bench for a breather. Of course, I knew all about the cardinal rule — you don't mention shutout to a goalie but when Junkin came over, I said, "C'mon, Joe. Keep it up. You got a shutout going. Don't blow it now. Don't choke, Joe!"

Fifteen seconds later they scored on him. Well, Joe was sick. He came out of the nets, skated over to the bench, told me to bug off and then skated back to the net.

I got my comeuppance after the game. We were in a hurry to get on the bus, so I decided to help carry out the bags. Normally we're not supposed to touch the equipment. That's the sacred province of the trainers, but this was a special situation. As I was leaving the dressing room two little kids looked up at me and one said to the other: 'I told you he didn't play with them. He's just a trainer or something.'"

Craig Ramsey's Forgotten Offside

I was playing for Buffalo along with Peter McNab, Rick Dudley and Brian Spencer. This particular game was at

Oakland and we had a line with McNab centering for Dudley and Spencer.

Duds and Spinner both were very intense guys who could get lost in thought and on this rush, their line was offside.

The linesman clearly blew his whistle but, somehow, Duds and Spinner didn't hear it and while everybody else on the ice stopped, they kept going as if there had never been a toot.

They circled around in the zone both with their head down and — pow! — they ran right smack into each other.

They both went flying and the collision was so hard that Dudley's headband flew right off his brow and the two of them were laying on the ice while the rest of us just roared with laughter.

Duds and Spinner finally came to their senses and lined up for the next face-off. It so happened that Duds was right next to the glass where there happened to be a cheerleader named Crazy George who would whoop up the crowd with a tambourine.

As soon as Duds got to his feet, Crazy George leaned over the glass and slammed his big tambourine in Dudley's ear.

Duds jumped right into the air and tried to attack Crazy George over the glass and, luckily, George got away.

Steve Tambellini Remembers the Stanley Cup Going to the Dogs

I played on the New York Islanders first Stanley Cup-winning team in 1980 and that was really something to behold, especially the celebrations we had after the championship was our's. The one party I remember above all was at Clark Gillies' house. Clarkie was our big left wing on the line with Bryan Trottier and Mike Bossy. He was a fun-loving guy who had the guys over to his house for a party.

Somebody managed to bring The Stanley Cup along in

all its shining splendor. In the middle of the party, Gillies remembered that he had to feed his dog, a huge German Shepherd. He filled the top of the Stanley Cup with dog food and the next thing I knew I was viewing an unbelievable sight; a huge dog having dinner out of The Stanley Cup!

I don't expect to see something like that again.

Peter Nedved Learns About Sundaes on Monday
Coming from overseas my English wasn't very good when I started playing hockey in Vancouver and that led to some funny mistakes.

I recall one road trip when we were in the East and the guys were having dessert at the hotel. One of the fellows had a nice big bowl of ice cream with all kinds of sweet stuff on it.

"What is that?" I asked.

"A sundae," he told me.

I tried to remember that for future use and, sure enough, the next day I happened to see a Dairy Queen and went in for some ice cream.

When the lady asked me what I wanted, I tried very hard to remember what I had been told the day before but all I could remember was a day.

Finally, I said, "Miss, could you give me a Monday ice cream."

She looked at me as if I was joking; which I was not.

Pat Quinn's Near Boston Massacre

In April 1969 I was a young Toronto defenseman on a not-very-good Maple Leaf team. This was the second year of NHL expansion, going from six to twelve teams, and it was at the time that Bobby Orr was coming into his own as the league's greatest defenseman.

Orr was in his third year with the Bruins and he already was regarded as a god to Boston fans, and I do mean GOD. The Boston Garden crowd regarded him as some kind of saint and woe to the opponent who messed around with Bobby.

Well, we were into our opening game of the first play off round, Toronto vs.Boston at the Garden and the Bruins were handling us pretty good (final score 10-0 for Boston). That wasn't going to stop me from doing my thing, which meant hitting as many Bruins as possible, which I did.

On one of Orr's rushes up the ice, he made the mistake of keeping his head down just as he reached my patch of ice. I don't know that he ever saw me but I caught him a terrific check and knocked Bobby unconscious.

It was a perfectly clean check but I wound up getting a penalty anyway and headed for the penalty box. By the time I got there all hell had broken loose. Bruins fans were up in arms because Orr was stretched out and looked liked he was really hurt.

When I got to the the penalty box, I was attacked by I don't know how many fans and even hit over the head by one of them. When I turned around to see what was happening, there was a whole sea of people trying to get at me.

My only "protector" was a solitary cop in the penalty box with me. When I saw all those angry faces trying to get me, I instinctively put my stick up to protect myself. When I did that, the cop grabbed a hold of me and we jostled around the box busting the glass barrier with the cop getting all cut up in the process.

At that point there was a full-scale panic on and with the sight of blood, I dove out of the box on to the ice to get away from everything. Luckily, I got an escort to the dressing room although a lot of Bruins fans were after my scalp.

We had to play the Bruins the very next night at Boston Garden and this time Orr was out of the lineup because of his concussion from my bodycheck.

I don't have to tell you that the place was wild; some 14,000 screaming fans some of whom had hung life-sized Pat Quinn mannequins in effigy. Still, I escaped without any damage although I can't say the same for our club. We got thrashed again, this time, 7-0, and left Boston with an aggregate two-game loss of 17-0!

After licking our wounds, we prepared to charter back to Toronto where the series would resume. Since I was one of the younger players on the team, my responsibility was to get some beer for the veterans. I finished dressing, left the Garden and walked down the street to the nearest tavern, which just happened to be Jack Sharkey's Bar, about five doors down from the front doors of Boston Garden.

I edged my way through the big crowd toward the bar to get some six-packs and was about half-way in when someone shouted, *"THERE'S PAT QUINN!"*

Was I ever scared. I mean here I was right in the middle of a wild bunch of Bruins' fans — with no escape. I thought I was in for big trouble but then I realized that it was Sharkey's place and most of the patrons were Irish like me.

Instead of hanging me in effigy — or just plain hanging me for real — they bought me an arm full of beer and clapped me on the shoulder and sent me off.

To this day, I really believe that only an Irishman in Boston could have gotten away with that.

Pat Elynuik Remembers Terry Simpson's Running Gag

Before Simpson came to the NHL as coach of the New York Islanders, he was one of the best Junior coaches in Canada.

I played for Terry when he had the Prince Albert (Saskatchwan) Raiders. Simpson was king of the town and ran a very tight ship with the hockey club.

We won a lot of games when I played there but we lost a few, too, and I can remember the road losses in particular because of what Simpson would do.

There were times after we were defeated in an away game when he would force the players to RUN behind the team bus from the arena all the way to our hotel.

And if you think that was tough, just remember that we had to do it *wearing all our hockey equipment!*

Can you imagine him trying that in the NHL?

Phil Housley's Idea of Unfair Playfair

When I was with Buffalo, the Sabres had a defenseman, Larry Playfair, who didn't play very fair when it came to messing around with our equipment.

He was apt to pull any one of three tricks on the boys:

1. Cutting a player's hockey blade from his supply of sticks, taping up the blade to cover up the breakage and putting the stick back in the pile for the fateful moment when the player would need his stick.

2. Putting Vaseline on the upper shafts of teammates' sticks.

3. Snipping the laces on player's boots before they'd leave the dressing room for practice. This would force the player to return to the room for a new set of laces and that,

in turn, would cause the player to be late for the scrimmage, which would lead to the player catching heck from the coach.

Rick Ley's Unforgettable Opening Game

The World Hockey Association made its debut in October 1972 and while some teams did very well for a start, others had some rocky moments. I can tell you about the Philadelphia Blazers because I was there.

My club was the New England Whalers and we were playing out of Boston Garden in the first WHA year, 1972-73. Compared to some other clubs we were very well-organized and, of course, played in first-rate Boston Garden, which was the Bruins' home as well.

It was different for other teams. Philadelphia's WHA team was called the Blazers and they would not play in the Flyers' home rink, The Spectrum. Instead, they opted for a place called Convention Hall which had about 10,000 seats and was supposed to be all set for hockey.

Trouble is, nobody told that to the ice-making machinery.

We got to the arena for the Blazers' debut and there were all sorts of pre-game ceremonies planned as befitting a new team in a new league.

That was the good news. The bad news was that the ice-maker couldn't make ice. By game time, there still was a band six inches long around the boards with nothing but sand instead of ice.

Because there were so many people in the building, the new management wanted to play the game anyway so they got the Zamboni machine out for one more run around the ice.

Wouldn't you know it, the driver put the Zamboni right through the end of the rink, which guaranteed that we wouldn't be able to play.

Meanwhile, Derek Sanderson, who was the million-dollar star of the Blazers had to take over the microphone and explain what had happened.

When the Philadelphia fans heard that the game was going to be cancelled, they pelted Sanderson with orange pucks that had been given away that night.

What an opening.

Guy Lafleur Remembers an Unwanted pair of Bermuda Shorts

When I played for the Canadiens there were two funny people I always had to watch out for because they had no end of pranks. I'm talking about big Peter Mahovlich and Jimmy Roberts.

They would do anything to loosen up guys before a game, laughing all the time.But you never knew when they would strike and, even though I tried to be careful, they got me good one day, cutting my pants at the knees.

Since I didn't have another pair of trousers around, I had no choice but to return home with my pants looking like a pair of Bermuda shorts.

Hall of Famer Ted Lindsay's Most Memorable Character
During the 1950s when the Montreal Canadiens won five straight Stanley Cups,the Habs had a lot of big names like Rocket Richard, Jean Beliveau and Doug Harvey. But they also had a second-stringer who used to get a fair amount of ink.

He was a Frenchman, Marcel Bonin, who was a rugged sonofagun and not a bad player at that. But Bonin had a claim to fame that I never heard from any other hockey player; as a hobby he would wrestle bears and chew glass.

When he was a rookie, Marcel had a problem with English, especially when he was on the road and had to order meals.

Somebody told Marcel that he couldn't go wrong if he told the waitress, "Give me an order of ham-and-eggs."

The next morning he ordered ham-and-eggs for breakfast and it worked out fine. So he ordered ham-and-eggs for lunch and dinner and this went on for two months — until he learned some new words like steak, potatoes and lamb chops.

The Drop Kick Bob Daily Will Never Forget
Goalies are funny guys and not too many will top Gary (Suitcase) Smith. He had this thing about placekicking. One of his safety valve pastimes was placekicking shoes over signs while he was waiting in airline terminals. He loved drop kicking and would even practice drop-kicking the puck during scrimmages.

When I played with him in Vancouver during the early 1970's, he pulled a kicking routine while we were skating against Toronto at Maple Leaf Gardens.

This was during a Leaf power play and we were doing our best to kill the penalty. Somehow the puck got away from the Leafs and slid right down to Suitcase. Instead of clearing it, he skated with the puck all the way to the blue line. When he got there, Gary did the craziest thing you ever saw; he drop-kicked the puck over everybody.

As the puck went sailing through the air, Leafs defenseman Jim McKenny — another funny guy — put his arms up in the air like a football referee watching a field goal attempt, and screamed, "IT'S GOOD!"

Ed Hospodar's Mistaken Applause

When I joined the Rangers as a rookie, not many people knew me and my style wasn't exactly conducive to standing ovations. That's why I was surprised when I played my first game at Madison Square Garden. When I stepped on the ice with Ron Greschner and Phil Esposito, the place immediately launched a huge cheer. Esposito leaned over and said, "Eddie, that cheer is for you."

For a few seconds I believed him and was feeling great about myself until I turned around and noticed that the great Bobby Hull had just skated out for Hartford. It was The Golden Jet's first game in New York as a Whaler and THAT was why the crowd was going crazy, not for me.

The Most Unusual Post-Practice Observation

"I love the smell of lactic acid in the morning!"
— *Bob Berry*

(Lactic acid is produced when the body burns carbohydrates, something that happens in abundance during severe hockey workouts.)

Ron Caron's Slide Under the Bench Routine

Before I became an executive with the St.Louis Blues, I worked for the Montreal Canadiens organization as a scout and then, in 1988, I was general manager of the Montreal Voyageurs of the American Hockey League. Our player-coach was defenseman Al MacNeil but since we wanted him to concentrate on playing, I got behind the bench a few times.

In my first road game we were playing at Providence and leading, 3-1. I had Bob Berry on the bench for five or six shifts because he had taken an early bad penalty, which I didn't like.

At the eight minute mark of the third period, I said to Bob, "Can you give me a good shift here, 35 seconds, and not take a stupid penalty?"

He said sure he could and out he went on the next shift. Well, Berry was out about 20 seconds when the referee blew his whistle for a penalty against Bob.

I got so mad, I kicked and I slid and I went right UNDER the bench.

The guys didn't know what had happened. One of them said, "Where are you coach?"

I was not there.

Three NHLers on the Most Unusual Thing They've Seen on the Ice

Neil Broten: When I played for the University of Minnesota, we were known as The Golden Gophers. On road trips to the University of North Dakota the Dakota fans would throw dead gophers on the ice at the beginning of the game, in between periods and just about any time there's a whistle. Real, dead gophers and I haven't any idea where they got them.

Derian Hatcher: When I played Junior hockey for North Bay, we'd visit the London (Ontario) club and their fans would rub it in when they beat us. Once they threw three

chickens on the ice and another time a big, bag of groceries. Don't ask me why groceries, but there they were. And it was a BIG bag.

Brian Glynn: During my stint in the International League, I played for Salt Lake City and once we had a game in Peoria. Their club was known as the Rivermen and apparently some fan pulled something out of the river because after Peoria scored a goal this great, big, ugly thing appeared on the ice. It looked like a cross between an octopus and a squid and all I remember is the officials scrambling around, trying to find something to pick the creature up with to get it off the ice.

Bob Plager's Favorite Barclay Plager Story
When Barclay and I played for the St.Louis Blues, he made a point of saying that he didn't want to take the game home

with him, which was understandable. His approach was that hockey should not be discussed in the house.

What would happen is that I would come visit him and let him know that I had a hockey problem. He'd say, "I'll meet you at the corner bar."

We must have talked hockey twenty times a day.

Hall of Famer Milt Schmidt's Most Memorable Character
During the 1930's there was a French-Canadian player named Jean Baptiste Pusie who played for the Canadiens, Rangers and Bruins for short periods of time. Most fellows took the game seriously but Pusie was an exception; he had an act out there.

When he was with us, he once bet $10 — a lot of money in 1936 — that he would get all his hair cut off. Nobody would believe that a hockey player would do that right in the middle of the season but Pusie took the ten bucks and came back with all his hair cut off!

There were times when he was awarded a penalty shot, which is another serious moment in a game. But not for Pusie. The first thing he would do was skate up to the opposition goaltender, pat him on the back, wish him well and then return to center ice for the shot. In my mind he was the funniest character of all.

Mike Richter on Lindy Ruff
When Lindy Ruff played for the Rangers, he didn't get a whole lot of ice time but he sure made his presence felt off the ice. There was no better practical joker and, further-more, Lindy took pride in his ability to sneak in and sew someone's pocket shut.

He got me good one day after learning of my reputa-tion for being a little bit cheap.

When I wasn't around, Lindy somehow got into my locker and found my wallet. I had a couple of $20 bills and about ten $1 bills. He glued them all together and returned them to the wallet so that there was no way of my knowing that it had been disturbed.

After the practice, I got dressed, put my wallet in my pocket and took off. A day later I was driving to the rink and stopped at a toll booth. There I am trying to hand the clerk money and all I could do is hand him a wad of bills that wouldn't come apart.

Ruff had all sorts of tricks. He happened not to like a new pair of shoes I had bought so when I wasn't looking, he nailed them to a wooden bench. A few minutes later I was ready to put the shoes on, reached for them and, whoops! I got a whole bench for my efforts.

Practical jokers like Lindy spare nobody, not even new-comers to the team. I remember when we acquired defenseman Randy Moller from Quebec. He met the club during a stop in Winnipeg for a game with the Jets.

Moller went into the dressing room to put on his equipment in order to get a skate with the team before the game. As he walked out on to the ice, he tried to pull his zipper out in the cold air. He's walking out but he can't get the thing up. Lindy had turned his pants inside out and sewed his zipper down. Man, that guy was good with the needle and thread!

Jeff Chychrun's Favorite Story

Sometimes before a game, a player would crack smelling salts to get himself going. One day our veteran defenseman on the Flyers, Mark Howe, decided to pull one on one of our rookies, Greg Smythe. He said to him, "Smitty, you're so big and tough, I remember a guy around here who used to crack them open IN HIS NOSE."

Smythe took Howe seriously. He actually grabbed one smelling salt vial, put it in his nostril and then cracked it. Next thing we knew, he fainted.

Andy Moog's Favorite Story
We were playing the Vancouver Canucks and the game got a bit rough. The referee was Paul Stewart and when one of our players got cross checked from behind in front of the Canucks' net, I expected a penalty to be called, especially since he was looking right at the play.

There was no call.

I was fuming and when play came down to my end of the rink, I told Stewart that he blew the call.

"That call sucks!" I shouted.

Stewart looked at me for a second and then gave me a ten minute misconduct penalty.

When I heard that, I screamed, "AND THAT SUCKS, TOO!!"

Rick Tocchet's Favorite Story
When I played for the Philadelphia Flyers we once played a trick on two rookies on the team. They were looking for a bar to go to and the guys suggested one that we said they probably would like. What we neglected to tell them was that it had a reputation for being a gay bar.

Of course, they didn't have a clue so they took off and went to the place. As it turned out there happened to be a couple of girls there but about 20 men.

What did the rookies know — nothing. They sat down and had a couple of beers, talked a little and had a few more. After a while the men in the joint got up and started dancing, holding and grabbing one another.

The rookies started looking around and saw what was happening, picked themselves up and got out as fast as their legs could carry them. The unbelievable part is that they stayed there for two hours before they realized what we had put them up to with the gag.

A Few Gems from Marshall Johnston

Better known for his baseball ownership of the Oakland Athletics, Charles Finley also was a hockey entrepreneur but for a much shorter time. The eccentric millionaire was one of a long line of Oakland Seals owners and though he spent but a few years in hockey, Finley made an indelible imprint.

One of his players was Marshall Johnston, currently director of player personnel for the New Jersey Devils. Johnston sat down with us one afternoon at Byrne Meadowlands Arena and reminisced about playing for the flaky Finley.

A lot of people put the knock on Finley calling him off-the-wall and stuff like that but, actually, I liked the guy even though he did some wild things. One thing was certain; if we won for him, the world was our oyster.

I can remember the Seals going into Boston as big underdogs and beating the Bruins. Our next game was in New York City and Charlie trekked us all down to fashionable Fifth Avenue and bought us all expensive new shoes at Gucci's. Another time after a win, we came home to Oakland and Charlie took us to a nice outfitter and bought the bunch of us Kelly green blazers, black slacks, the works.

On the other hand, Finley could be rough. There was a time when one of our teammates talked anonymously about Charlie with someone from the Oakland Tribune. I mean he really blasted the boss and the next day we're on the plane with Finley and he calls a meeting. He pounded the table and said, "All right, which of you red-blooded Americans is gonna own up to saying this?"

It was obviously someone in the room but nobody said a word. Charlie backed off a bit and nothing more was heard about it. But since I was the player rep, I wanted to talk with him about my own concerns. For example, he would fly us first class — which was pretty nice — but it wasn't helping us win game, because the guys would take advantage of the free booze on those five-hour flights between New York and Oakland.

Finley is famous — or is it infamous? — for having players wear white skates at a time when NHL players would only wear the traditional black boots. This was quite a shock to some of the players and we'd get needled quite a bit on road trips. Fans would say, "Hey, where's your nice, white purse to go with your nice white skates?"But in California the fans thought the white skates were neat.

Finley came up with the white skates just to be different but people would come up with all sorts of oddball theories to justify them. Once I was listening to a hockey telecast and one announcer said to the other, "Why would they go to white skates?" The other guy said, "It's gotta be because when the puck's in the corner and everyone on the other team wears black skates, it's hard to see the puck. But if you've got white skates on..."

Listening to that, I leaped up and said, "Shit, I'd never thought of that!" I almost fell out a my chair thinking there actually might be a sensible reason for wearing white boots.

But I knew Finley and I knew that he just wanted to be different. He did the same with the Oakland Athletics baseball uniforms. Why he once tried to persuade the NHL to switch from the black to a flourescent puck. He used to tell me, "When I watch hockey on the tube I can never follow the damn puck; I don't know why we don't have an orange puck out there; it would be a lot easier to follow."

Guess what? He might be right.

Finley's coach was a fellow named Fred (No Kid) Glover who had had a fantastic minor league career as a forward but never could make an impact in the NHL and this bothered him no end. Freddie was a hard-nosed character who played hard at everything, even practices. A Glover practice was really a scrimmage and he would make sure that he played on one of the teams — and whatever side he was on HAD to win. After a while we got the message and we'd make sure that his side won so we wouldn't have to be out there for two-and-a-half hours.

The Seals never won anything big but they sure had their share of characters.One was a goalie named Gary

Smith who was nicknamed Suitcase because he always seemed to be packing to move on to yet another team. Suitcase was a darn good goalie but one night he really shook up the coach. He was playing for a guy named Frank Mario who had a habit of opening a game by tossing the puck to the goalie who always sat on the bench for a few minutes before taking the ice.

So, Smitty is sitting there and Mario says, "Okay, you ready, Smitty?" And Frank throws him the puck; a nice soft toss and whaddya know, Smitty, the great goalie, misses it completely. What a way to start a game.

Suitcase's brother, Brian, was another piece of work. I played alongside him in Minnesota and neither of us was getting much ice. When the buzzer sounded ending the first period, Brian said, "Follow me!" and led me on to the ice. He began skating alongside the Zamboni machine until I finally said, "What the hell are you doing?"

Well in those days none of the hockey tv shows had intermissions so the camera would following the Zamboni. "Don't you understand," Smitty said, "this is our way of getting on tv!"

One of the most excitable guys I ever played for was Wren Blair when we were in Minnesota. To drum up interest in those early expansion days, the team would often hold practices in suburban rinks and sometimes we'd draw 400 to 500 people. One day Blair was putting us through a drill and finally blew his whistle and called us over to the boards. "You guys aren't skating today," he yelled. "I want to see some work out a ya!" And with that he threw his stick against the boards.

Now that had to be a one in a million thing. The stick shattered on impact but it ricocheted right back at Wren and catches him right in the eye. So there he was in a new white jacket, blood splattered all over it and we players were going crazy.

Blair was not an easy man to bargain with no matter how good the player might be. He once had a guy who scored 50 goals and was bragging about it to Wren. To which Blair shot back, "It's the ones after 50 that count!"

Chapter Ten

HUMOR
HOT OF THE ICE

Considering the intensity which the game generates it is remarkable that hockey has produced so many laughs. Perhaps it is a result of the unique blend of beauty and violence which constitutes the essence of hockey and explains why there are an equal amount of laughs to go with the yelling and screaming.

The contrast is equally evident in the players; extraordinarily tough players over the years — such as Lou Fontinato, John Ferguson and Nick Fotiu were veritable lambs off the pond.

Products of the robust Canadian north, hockey players as a rule have always betrayed a frontier brand of spirit and this, in and of itself, has made an imprint on the humor of the sport.

Hockey gags come in various shapes and forms, involving the very biggest names to the lowliest assistant trainers. Over the years it has not changed much and. despite the fanaticism of the pasttime and the pressure cooker air about the game, a significant number of laughs always emerge.

For example, during an exhibition game in New Haven between the Rangers and the Bruins, a Boston rookie was hit flush in the face with an errant shot, and was helped off the ice. When the doctor escorted the player to the dressing room, they were greeted by a Bruins veteran dressed in his "civvies." The vet peered at the long, bleeding cut with interest. The doctor glanced first at the rookie, then at the battle-scarred veteran without saying a word. All was quiet. Finally the old pro calmly lit a cigar and without a flicker of emotion, said softly to the doctor, "Put an ASPIRIN on it and send him back, doc!"

In the same early September game, the jam-packed arena was so warm that FOG formed over the playing surface, sometimes so thick that it obliterated the players from the fans' view. Time and time again the referee stopped the game to have the players skate around the perimeter of the rink to "blow" the fog away! Every three minutes, the action would stop and the players would go "for a skate" to disperse the fog.

"Gump" Worsley, then a Ranger goalie, took the opportunity to display his humor.

When Boston launched a three-on-one attack into Ranger territory, the Gumper skated out of the crease and HID behind the net! Naturally, the Bruins scored. Later, in the dressing room, Worsley was asked what had prompted him to play "hide and seek." Gump replied: "I'm just too valuable to be hurt in a game like this!" Then, getting to his feet and padding towards the showers, he added, "Besides, I figured Jack The Ripper would come out of the fog and assault me!"

Another time, in an Eastern League game, the Johnstown Jets were the best skating team, featuring the dipsy-do of Dick Roberge, a leading scorer in the circuit. With the Jets leading New Haven in the second period, 8-0, and the New Haven fans hollering for blood -- or at least a better showing, Roberge skated through the porous Blade defense for the umpteenth time that night and scored his fifth goal!

On the bench, the New Haven coach saw the futility of the situation, and also the humor, as a plan fashioned itself in his mind. The next time Roberge wound up behind his own net for another rink-length dash, the coach EMPTIED HIS BENCH, sending ALL 14 men on the ice! Naturally, the referee blew the whistle for a penalty and the fans immediately quieted down. Asked by the official to explain his actions, the coach replied with a wide grin, "I just wanted to see if the SOB could skate through my ENTIRE team and score!" Even the referee smiled at that one!

Before the advent of Herculite glass surrounding the ice surface, players were sometimes chucked over the boards and into the laps of fans. During a game at Madison Square Garden in the '50's, Gaye Stewart of the Rangers was dumped over the boards by Ernie Dickens of the Black Hawks...right into the lap of a portly gentleman drinking beer. Seated next to the man was a lovely young lady who was shocked to find a player next to her. The beer went one way, and Stewart, always with an eye for beauty, gallantly planted a kiss on the young woman's cheek, gently helped the man from the floor and, reeking with the aroma of spilled beer, hurdled the boards and resumed play! Some of us in the press box suggested that the least Stewart could have done was order another beer for the fan!

During a Calder Cup playoff game in the Rhode Island Auditorium some 30 years ago between the Reds and the visiting Pittsburgh Hornets, "Wild Bill" Ezinicki had lots of fun at the expense of the Providence fans.

Providence was being outclassed and out-muscled by the likes of Ezinicki, Rudy Migay, Tim Horton and a few other future Toronto Stars. The fans, showing their displeasure, showered the ice with heated pennies which instantly melted holes and stuck fast in the ice. Again and again play was stopped to pry money from the ice. Even after repeated appeals the fans continued to fling money. Ezinicki solved the officials' dilemma. He confiscated a woman's purse, hopped onto the ice and and pried the pennies from the ice, dropping them into a handbag! Then, blowing kisses to the crowd, Ezinicki blithely skated back to the bench amidst cheers from the Hornets! that stopped the money throwing, but we never discovered whether Ezinicki kept the money or not!!!

Fights on the ice are sometimes bitter and quite serious,

yet they are more often an icebound version of the Keystone cops.

In an Eastern League game in the early 1960's, both benches emptied for a free-for-all. Gloves and sticks were strewn all over the ice and players were paired off from blue line to blue line, pummeling, punching, and wrestling. At the rear of the action stood a massive defenseman from one team, and a few feet away, the tiny forward of the opposing team, neither anxious to go at the other. Suddenly, the defenseman grabbed the small forward in his arms and wrestled him to the ice, shouting: "I'll take this guy...and a player to be named AT A LATER DATE!" Everyone broke up...and peace was restored.

After the start of World War II the New York Rangers had trouble fielding a competitive team, since most of their stars had been drafted or enlisted in the armed forces. Montreal, however, had a great club with Maurice Richard, Elmer Lach, Butch Bouchard and others. At the start of the season Phil Watson, star center for the Rangers, failed to obtain a visa to cross the Canadian American border to play. so the Rangers traded him for the season to Montreal in return for Dutch Hiller, a thin, fast skating, non-belligerent forward.

The Rangers had played a Saturday night game in Montreal, losing by a decisive margin. In that game, Leo Lamoreaux, a big, bruising Montreal defenseman, and Bryan Hextall, the Rangers ace scorer, titled in a lengthy fight. When the teams met the next night in New York both players went at it again, only this time just pushing and shoving. Play was stopped as the linesman tried to restore decorum.

Meanwhile, on the other side of the rink, Hiller, skating up and down and anxiously awaiting the resumption of play, started to become more and more angry with the delay. At last he skated to the spot where Lamoreaux and Hextall were being held apart. Hiller slid between a linesman and Lamoreaux, and without any preliminaries, spun the defenseman around and with ONE PUNCH, dropped the Montrealer to the ice.

Hextall was suitably astonished and so were the linesman and the referee. In fact everyone on the ice — including Dutch Hiller — was stunned by the belligerence of the non-belligerent Hiller. All he wanted to do was get the game going again, but in the heat of the moment he kayoed Lamoreux, who outweighed him by 40 pounds. What then, were the officials to do? The referee gave Hiller a two-minute penalty for interference. Meanwhile, Lamoreux skated off the ice, laughing.

A constant source of humor, first during his years as a Ranger player and later as coach was Phillipe Henri (Phil) Watson. One of Watson's problems which lent itself to humor — was his failure to master the English language. Once when he wanted to ridicule an older player by calling him a "has-been," Watson snapped at the foe: "You're nothing but a BEEN HAS!"

Because of his trigger temper, Watson frequently was embroiled in fights with the foe and these, in turn, often produced laughs — usually at Phil's expense.

Once, Watson had a feud with Chicago Blackhawks defenseman Earl Siebert, a hulking, slow moving behemoth almost twice Watson's size. Phil was frustrated in his attempts to get at Siebert but finally the situation presented itself. Prying the puck away from the boards, Siebert had his back to center ice.

Seeing his enemy was vulnerable, Watson took six or seven long, powerful strides from the blue line, going full tilt at Siebert. As the Ranger streaked at him, big Earl turned slightly and spotted Watson bearing down. Siebert waited until the last split second to step aside. Watson couldn't change direction as quickly and crashed face-first into the boards, collapsing to the ice, dazed and bleeding.

Ever so solicitous, Siebert helped the fallen Ranger to his skates and after the whistle had blown, escorted him to the bench. Siebert gently patted Watson's backside as if to say, "Better luck next time!" Not surprisingly, Watson never went after Siebert again.

Sportswriters occasionally become involved in the humor of hockey. Once, in New Haven, a hometown writer repeatedly blasted the skating abilities of one of the players, until the player was fed up to here. Since the columnist was small and frail, the player couldn't physically take him to task, so he decided to do it with laughs. The players skated on to the ice with the rest of the team for the pre-game warm up, wearing DOUBLE RUNNERS! When he spotted the writer, he shouted in the direction of the press box: "Maybe this will help, eh!" Instantly, the press box erupted with laughter, making it so uncomfortable for the critical scribe that he stopped his attacks and settled down to simply reporting what happened on the ice.

In each arena there always seems to be a fan with a precious sense of the twit and the pun. Once when King Clancy refereed in the NHL a Boston Garden regular would constantly shout. "King, you remind me of a town in Massachusetts — MARBLEHEAD!"

During a game at Madison Square Garden in the early 1970's Rangers winger Dave Balon got some advice from a New York fan. It was a hard-checking game against the big, bad Bruins. Balon had four great chances to score, but his shots were weak and easily pushed aside by Gerry Cheevers in the Boston nets. A few minutes later, taking a beautiful pass from teammate Walt Tkaczuk, Balon skated in on Cheevers alone but, once more, he flubbed the shot.

Way upstairs a fan screamed down: Hey, Balon, you bum, send him a TELEGRAM! It'll get there FASTER!" Speaking of telegrams, the Canadian comedy team of Johnny Wayne and Frank Shuster were long time fans of the Toronto Maple Leafs. As a gag, the comics once dis-patched a telegram to then Leafs' major domo, George (Punch) Imlach, and signed it with the names of the Maple Leaf Gardens Board of Directors. The Message read: "PUNCH — WE'RE WITH YOU ALL THE WAY, WIN OR TIE!"

Many a hockey laugh has been enjoyed over the subject of absenteeism; players who fail to report to duty on time, or miss practices or training camp -- or both. Howie Young, who once played defense for the Chicago Blackhawks and Detroit Red Wings, was once the most notorious, if not hilarious, missing person among the NHL skaters.

Young's antics eventually led to his departure from the NHL but not before he pulled off a gem of a disappearing act after last being seen in the lobby of Chicago's La Salle Street railway station and evaporating in broad daylight. When Young came up for air, the Black Hawks gave him a one-way ticket to Los Angeles and it was there, in the land of the stars, that Howie continued his bizarre antics. He was offered a bit part in a Frank Sinatra movie and, in a moment of whimsy, he supposedly dropped "Old Blue Eyes" into the ocean from the deck of a yacht. With that the film makers asked Young to leave, again. (Sinatra, 'tis said, couldn't swim.)

When Howie played for Detroit, he roomed with the veteran defenseman Bill Gadsby. One afternoon, the pair checked into their hotel room for their pre-game nap. Gadsby was lying in bed, reading, when Young appeared, dressed to the nines in a Madison Avenue suit, topped with a sharp hat and bottomed with a pair of cowboy boots. Young nonchalantly removed his coat and hat and, just as calmly, dropped them on the floor. Then he unbuttoned his jacket, removed his tie, and offhandedly tossed them on the carpet. "I thought I saw everything," said Gadsby, "until Howie sat on the bed and slipped off his cowboy boots. Instead of throwing them in the pile on the floor, he took them in hand and daintily placed them on the dresser -- like valuable diamonds."

Another classic of absenteeism was experienced by Hec Fowler, a goalie for the Victoria Cougars, the Boston Bruins and other pro clubs. Seems that Fowler's problem was that he was an ardent fire buff. "On at least two occasions," wrote Toronto columnist Jim Coleman, "The opening face-off for a game was delayed because Fowler hadn't arrived at the rink — he had followed the fire engines and was supervising efforts to control the conflagration."

Sometimes absenteeism is excusable. Bob Davidson, the NHL scout who was a first rate left-winger for the Toronto Maple Leafs, once had the best excuse of all. He was playing at Montreal's Forum on a line with Ted (Teeder) Kennedy. There was a face off in the Canadiens end of the rink. Kennedy moved into the face-off circle and then peered to his right, checking his right wing, and then his left. When Kennedy looked to his left, he did a double take. Davidson was gone!

Sure enough, Davidson was absent; but with good reason: a pair of Montreal fans had yanked the left wing over the boards and were wrestling with him in the aisle behind the rail seats!

Not surprisingly, Jean Baptiste Pusie, one of pro hockey's most irrepressible clowns, was involved in an absentee act once. It developed after a particularly obnoxious fan was giving him the business. Pusie leaped over the boards and went after his tormentor. The fan fled from the rink

but the determined Pusie pursued the spectator. The fan
ran down the street with Pusie, still wearing his skates,
losing ground steadily. After two or three blocks, Pusie
said "to hell with it" and, instead of returning to the rink, he
dropped into a bar to have a short beer.

A fight that confined itself to the rink proved most
interesting one night at Maple Leaf Gardens when Alex
Levinsky of Toronto and Nels Stewart of the Montreal
Maroons started swinging. They scuffled behind the Leaf
goal. Stewart threw his right fist at Levinsky, but it collided,
instead, with a goal post.

Stewart skated to the Montreal bench and, holding his
damaged right paw, said to Maroons coach Odie Cleghorn:
"Migawd, Odie, I think it's broke."

"So, what?" barked Cleghorn, "Your left hand's Okay,
isn't it? G'wan back there and fight!"

Misery on ice frequently inspires humor. One of the
most miserable teams of the 1950's was the Chicago
Blackhawks, yet when Tommy Ivan took over as the Windy
city's general manager, he found that a loser can produce a
giggle here and there. During the previous season the
Hawks had produced only 31 points, so when the new
training camp opened, Ivan figured he would encounter a
win-thirsty group of athletes ready for the rigors of a
heavy workout.

Ivan was rather stunned when he spoke with his
charges.

"The first six men I talked to," said Ivan, "wanted raises.
So after the first half dozen came in with their requests, I
called the entire team together.

"'Look, I said, 'last year we got only 31 points. We
finished dead last. Today I find that the first six guys I talk
to felt they deserved raises. Now, with only 31 points,
somebody must have played badly.'"

With that, one of the Blackhawks piped up: "Maybe we
looked at it this way: the team played bad, but we played
good."

Losers, the injured and weaker players of the game

refined their sense of humor as a defense against their oppressor — the winners, the healthy and the big skaters. One who was especially sharp in this department was Camille (The Eel) Henry, the elusive but awfully skinny left wing who played for the New York Rangers during his prime in the late 1950's.

To some, Henry appeared to be a tragic figure. His attempts to add ounces — pounds were out of the question — to his fragile frame went for nought. One summer, Ranger Manager Murray (Muzz) Patrick prescribed a diet of malted milks for Henry. The Eel diligently obeyed the menu but, when training camp rolled around, he was as skinny as he had been in the pre-malted days.

Because of his almost lighter-than-air appearance, Henry was not one to throw many body checks. Once, Camille was questioned after a game in which he threw one of his rare checks. "Do you ever hurt anyone with those checks?" a writer asked Henry.

"Sure," he replied with a perfectly straight face. "Plenty of times."

"Whom do you hurt most?"

"Camille Henry."

Humor is a form of compensation and some of the best lines in hockey have emerged from severe situations, Punch Imlach, the spartan boss of the Toronto Maple Leafs, spawned many a laugh. Once, during Punch's early days at Maple Leaf Gardens he was showing films of games for review by his players. On this occasion, the movies were shown over and over again by Imlach to make a point. During a break in the showings Billy Harris (not related to the Harris who played for the Islanders in the 1970's) of the Leafs was approached by a newsman who encountered him in the Maple Leaf Gardens snack bar.

"What are you doing here," asked the reporter.

"It's intermission at the movies," quipped Harris "How's the film?" the other asked.

"Great," Harris replied. ""We're leading two nothing at the end of the second period, and I got to hurry back because, if I remember correctly, I think I get a goal and an assist in the third."

Although alcohol and ice go very well in cocktails, the mixture has been the bane of hockey managers since the invention of the game. Needless to say, the mixture also has produced its share of laughs and one-liners. Clint Benedict, the fine goaltender with the old Ottawa Senators, was responsible for just such a quip one day when his club was playing in Montreal. Although Benedict was not ordinarily a drinking man, he "got with some relatives" on this particular afternoon before the game and when he skated in goal at the Forum he was stiff. At first nobody noticed, but Montreal scored in a hurry and then got two more. Finally one of the Ottawa defenseman skated back and said: "Clint, what's the matter? That's three goals!"

"Three?" Benedict blurted. "When did they get the others?"

Booze was not a favorite of Marcel Bonin, who was an industrious left wing for the Montreal Canadiens and Detroit Red Wings, but glass and bears were. Bonin had perfected a stunt whereby he would chew glass and then devour it as one would a T-bone steak. Another of muscular Marcel's hobbies was wrestling with bears. Although he was an extrovert in these departments, Bonin, during his early hockey career, was terribly self-conscious about his inability to speak fluent English. This, purportedly, was the reason Marcel flopped in big-league tryouts with Detroit and Boston but was comfortable among the French-speaking Canadiens.

Hall Of Famer Doug Harvey, who teamed with Bonin on the Canadiens, recalled Marcel's uptight attitude on the road, where only English was spoken. "When we were travelling," said Harvey, "Bonin always arranged to eat with some English-speaking guy like me or Tom Johnson or Dickie Moore, Then, he'd study the menu, let whoever was with him order and when the waitress looked at him, Marcel would just say, "The Same!"

Booze frequently was on the minds of hockey players

during the prohibition and World War II days when (Wild) Bill Ezinicki was a Junior star with the Oshawa Generals, enroute to the Toronto Maple Leafs. Inadvertently the Polish-Canadian Ezinicki became involved in a strange story of lost hopes for liquor. "While I was playing for Oshawa," said Ezinicki, "one of the club officials decided to take me into Toronto to watch a Stanley Cup playoff game at Maple Leaf Gardens. He phoned ahead to Doug Laurie, a sporting goods dealer friend, to make sure he had tickets for us.

"The second World War was on. Among other things liquor was rationed. You were allowed a 12-ounce bottle a month. It was known as a "Mickey."

"'I'm bringing Ezinicki with me,' the Oshawa fellow told Laurie over the phone. That started it.

"Laurie thought he had said, 'I'm bringing a Mickey with me.' There were two or three thirsty friends of Doug's in the store at the time. He told them to stick around because a Mickey was on the way. It was like striking gold in those dry days.

"'Okay," Laurie greeted us, 'haul out the Mickey.'"

"'Who said anything about a Mickey? I told you I was bringing Ezinicki,' my friend told him.

Laurie and his pals almost cried. It was the near-breakup of a beautiful friendship. A Mickey was an important package. Certainly a lot more important than an Ezinicki!

But Booze was plentiful in the Roarin' Twenties when Ambrose Jason Moran and Spunk Sparrow played for the Regina Capitals. Once the pair was skating for the Caps against the Vancouver Maroons in a Stanley Cup elimination round. After the first game in Vancouver, Regina manager Wes Champ was counting the noses of his players as they boarded the train to go to the second game at Regina. Two noses were missing -- those noses belonged to Moran and Sparrow.

The playful pair always stoutly maintained that they had missed the train because they decided to go to the Vancouver Railroad station lunch room "to have a cup of coffee." According to hockey columnist Jim Coleman: "A search party which located the truants 12 hours later testified that the coffee must have had a high alcoholic content."

Bruins fans with good memories still chuckle over a fast one Boston manager Art Ross pulled on his counterpart, Lester Patrick, in the thirties. Seems that Ross figured the Old Madison Square Garden Rink was too cramped for his freewheeling Boston Bruins. What to do?

"Tell you what," Ross told his men in the dressing room before the game. "I want someone to go out there and punch Bill Cook right in the nose. That way we'll at least get a Ranger and a Bruin off the ice and we'll have more room."

The first to try was Red Beattie but he never could get to Cook before his turn was completed. Then there was a line change and this time Alex smith went over the boards and took dead aim at the high scoring right wing. Bop. Smith rapped Cook on the proboscis. Enraged, Bill's brother, Bun, dashed over to Smith and jumped him. By the time order was restored, Smith and the two Cooks each had themselves a penalty.

And, of course, Ross had the last laugh. Thanks to his ploy the Bruins won by a goal.

Needless to say, our abused friends, the referees, retain an excellent humor quotient, which is why they perform so capably. One of the funniest arbiters was Georges Gravel, a wonderful French Canadian who was as bald as a man could be bald. In fact, Gravel was as funny as he was hairless. Which was very.

A typical Gravel quip sputtered out in the middle of a Detroit Red Wing-Montreal Canadien game. Having failed to split the Montreal defense, a Detroit player pitched forward in a swan dive and lay face down on the ice hoping Gravel would give the Canadiens a penalty. But Georges was no fool.

He skated to the fallen athlete and laconically observed: "Why don't you get up? Don't you know you're melting the ice beneath you?

There are times when the people who pay to watch hockey games put on a better show than the players themselves. Observers differ as to which city has the wildest spectators in the NHL but those from Boston, Chicago and St. Louis rank at the top of the list.

For many years Bruins followers suffered through some of the worst hockey ever seen in an NHL city. Nevertheless, they still kept coming and, somehow, managed to retain their sense of humor. During the early sixties, when the Bruins were at their lowest ebb, the Boston sextet received "help" from an unexpected source.

On a Monday morning following the usual Sunday night Boston defeat, a fan named Sandy showed up at the then coach Milt Schmidt's office. "I want a tryout with the Bruins," he insisted. "I've seen your team play and I think I can make the club."

Schmidt wasn't about to dismiss a philanthropist without a hearing. "How old are you? Who have you played for? What makes you think you can play in the NHL?"

Sandy listened intently and then replied, "I can skate faster than anyone on the Bruins and I'll bet $10 on it."

Intrigued by the man's gall, Schmidt suggested that Sandy return home and pick up his skates. Yes, he was willing to accept the challenge.

Sandy showed up the following morning with a pair of skates that had not been sharpened for two years. Bruins trainer Dan Canney took care of that and then Sandy was ready to take the ice. "What's your position," asked Schmidt.

"Wing," said Sandy, So Schmidt decided to go along with the gag.

Murray Oliver, then the Bruins center, started a rush toward goalie Ed Johnston. Johnny Bucyk was on the left and Sandy was on the right. When they arrived to within ten feet of the goalie Oliver slipped a perfect pass to Sandy. Precisely at that moment, Johnston stepped aside, leaving nothing but an open net for the skating fan. Sandy took a swipe at it but missed the net and crashed into the end boards.